The
GOD
We Can Know

EXPLORING THE "I AM" SAYINGS
OF JESUS

ROB FUQUAY

ENLARGED-PRINT EDITION

UPPER
ROOM BOOKS®
NASHVILLE

Cover design: Marc Whitaker / MTWdesign
Interior typesetting: PerfecType, Nashville, TN
Cover photos: Jonathan Woon (sheep, grapes)
           Shutterstock.com (bread)

LIBRARY OF CONGRESS CATALOGING-IN-PUBLICATION DATA
Fuquay, Rob.
  The God we can know : exploring the "I am" sayings of Jesus, enlarged-print/ Rob Fuquay.
    pages cm
    ISBN 978-0-8358-1555-0 (print)—ISBN 978-0-8358-1339-6 (mobi)—ISBN 978-0-8358-1340-2 (epub)
1. Jesus Christ—Person and offices—Biblical teaching. 2. Jesus Christ—Knowableness—Biblical teaching. 3. God (Christianity)—Knowableness—Biblical teaching. I. Title.
  BT203.F87 2015
  232—dc23
                                                            2015016779

Printed in the United States of America

To my wife, Susan, and daughters Julie, Sarah, and Anna,
who encourage me to live out the motto of my home state:
esse quam videri, "to be rather than to seem."

CONTENTS

*See the accompanying children's, youth, and adult group guides
and supporting materials for this worship and study series at*
www.TheGodWeCanKnow.com

INTRODUCTION

Let us occupy ourselves entirely in knowing God.
The more we know [God] the more we will
desire to know [God].

—**Brother Lawrence**
The Practice of the Presence of God

I once went to a mountain-climbing school. Actually, my wife Susan sent me to a mountain-climbing school. I had taken an interest in alpine climbing but didn't really know what I was doing. Susan figured if I was going to risk my life it might be good to get some training. Besides, my life insurance wasn't paid up.

The next summer I traveled to the state of Washington where I spent a week on a glacier in the Cascades with a guide and two other "students." My fellow learners were a couple from New York City. Our experience began early in the morning when we were picked up outside our hotel in Seattle. We went first to a park where introductions took place, and we spread out our gear to make sure we all had what was needed. The next stop was a coffee shop before heading to the mountains.

Standing in line for coffee, the guy from New York, who was significantly bigger than me, turned around and said, "Okay, I understand you're a pastor. Is that right?" I could tell by his tone he was not excited about this possibility. I said, "As a matter of fact I am." He continued, "Well, let me get this straight right now. I don't want to hear a bunch of religious stuff all week. Got that? My girlfriend and I are on vacation, and we don't want to be preached to!"

I responded, "It's a deal. I'm on vacation and don't feel like preaching." He swallowed a shot of espresso like it was whiskey and then ordered an extra large dark roast. This was not someone to mess with! I would learn later that he was Jewish but not active in his faith. His girlfriend had never claimed any religious preference, and our guide had dabbled in many religious systems, currently Buddhism.

We got to the mountains, hiked the long trek to the glacier, and set up camp. Each day we spent ten to twelve hours learning climbing skills. During break times and lunches we sat on rocks and chatted, and the most curious thing happened. Spiritual conversations developed! Sometimes they started quite naturally while talking about the grandeur of the mountains and how they were created. Other times someone brought up an issue of violence in the news and wondered how God could allow such things to happen. Inevitably they would turn to me as the local expert on the topic of God and ask what I thought.

The most amazing episode, however, came on the last morning. For our "final exam" we would summit a local peak. Wake-up call was 2:00 A.M. After the hour-plus it took to eat and gear up, we roped ourselves together and prepared to climb. Right before we departed the guy from New York said, "*Wait!* Before we start we need the Rev to say a prayer." Yes, this was the same guy who threatened me five days earlier about preaching. I just about fell out of my harness! A prayer request—from this guy?

I regrouped, asked everyone to hold hands, and led us in prayer roped together and standing on the ice under a clear moonlit sky. I was reminded all over again that we all have yearnings. Deep yearnings. The kind of yearnings that make us wonder about life and this world and what it's all about. They're part of what binds us together. Even those of us disinterested in religion, and perhaps even faith, often wonder if there is a God; and if so, what does this God have to do with us? That is what this book is about.

This book is about knowing God and, more specifically, knowing God through Jesus. In many ways the Bible is a story of humanity's attempt to know God. Sometimes this effort is as obvious as the tower of Babel (Gen. 11:1-9). Other times the story describes people working hard to avoid God. Many passages in the Old Testament describe people's fear of what would happen if they saw God's face. It's as if we want to know God, but then we're not so sure.

The Bible also tells a story of God's desire to be known. The scriptures relate an unfolding drama of God's never-ending desire to come to us—of God's revealing. The highest expression of that desire is the gift of God's self in the person of Jesus.

John's Gospel records a collection of self-revealing statements by Jesus known as the "I Am" sayings. These statements, rich in imagery and steeped in historical meaning, provide powerful insights into the heart of God and God's desire to know and be known. In this book we'll explore those sayings with a threefold aim:

First, we want to understand the images Jesus uses to identify himself: bread, light, good shepherd, gate of the sheep, true vine, way of life, resurrection, and life. Appreciating the historical Jewish roots behind these images opens up a myriad of possible meanings.

Second, we want to discover how those broad meanings connect with our lives today. Jesus defined himself in the context of ordinary, everyday images people easily understood. We can translate these ancient images into applications for contemporary life. What does it mean to experience hunger or need guidance or desire security or want greater power for living? Better yet, how does a relationship with Jesus fulfill these needs? That is the purpose of the "I Am" sayings, which brings us to a third aim.

Even more than insight or application, taking these sayings to heart can bring us into closer connection with Jesus. Christianity is not a religion. It is a relationship. A living relationship requires nurture and attention. It is deepened with trust and respect. The "I Am" sayings of Jesus invite us into that kind of abiding relationship.

Think of this book as a journey into the world where Jesus spoke these sayings. Use all of your senses as you read. Visualize the landscape. Smell the sheep pens and the fresh bread (yes, I know those two aren't exactly compatible). Taste the fruit of the vine. Hear the voices of people in the stories. Feel the light and heat of the giant torches at the Temple as well as the bitter grief of Mary at the tomb of her brother. These images are meant to be experienced. God is in these experiences. They tell us that God can be known.

I hope you may be able to read this book as part of a small group experience in which you view related video segments filmed in the Holy Land. The videos are available on DVD with accompanying children's, youth, and adult group guides. Supporting materials for this worship and study series can be found at www.TheGodWeCanKnow.com. This study is ideal for use during the season of Lent, a time set apart for focusing on Jesus and knowing God better. But whether exploring the book and video with a group or simply reading this book with your imagination in gear, I invite you on this journey not only to know more *about* God but to *know* God yourself.

Order your coffee, strap on your pack, and let the journey begin.

1

Knowing the Great "I Am"

Exodus 3:1-14

God wants to be recognized.

Begin this study with that simple thought. God is not hiding. God doesn't avoid us. God wants to be known. That's the story of the Bible. God wanted to be known by Adam and Eve. They didn't have to look hard to find God. Even when they tried to hide, God came looking for them. God likes being recognized. God came to Abraham. Abraham recognized and welcomed God's presence; they had a special relationship. Abraham was called a friend of God. God came to the prophets so they could speak God's message to people: "I want to be recognized by you."

Eventually God stepped away from the script. God no longer used a spokesperson. God came directly to us in Jesus. Why? Because God wants to be known. Sure, God's presence is not always easy to recognize or feel. Even Jesus quoted the psalmist, "Why have you forsaken me?" (Matt. 27:46). God's presence is sometimes mysterious and difficult to understand. But if there is one overarching truth in scripture it is that God likes being recognized. God is always in motion coming our way. God can be known.

On several occasions in the Gospel of John, Jesus begins self-revealing statements with the words, "I am. . . ." They remind us of God's words to Moses on Sinai. While investigating a burning bush that wasn't consumed by the fire, Moses encounters God. God meets him on the mountain to give him a life-altering, history-changing mission. God calls Moses to liberate the people from bondage in Egypt.

But Moses said to God, "If I come to the Israelites and say to them,
'The God of your ancestors has sent me to you,' and they ask me,
'What is his name?' what shall I say to them?" God said to Moses,
"I AM WHO I AM." He said further, "Thus you shall say to the Israelites,
'I AM has sent me to you.'"

EXODUS 3:13-14

Thousands of years later Jesus declares "I am. . . ." He identifies himself with the God of Moses. Yet, he does more than identify. He reveals further truths of this God, this God we can know and who wants to know us.

In the following chapters we will look at the six most recognized "I Am" sayings of Jesus: Bread of Life; Light of the World; True Vine; Good Shepherd and Gate of the Sheep; the Way, the Truth, and the Life; and the Resurrection and the Life. The study before us will be a journey. Like any journey it requires openness to new encounters and experiences. I hope the chapters and group sessions will give you not only a fresh understanding of Jesus' words but also new ways to experience God's presence in your life. Before we examine them individually, let's think about the words "I Am" and what they tell us about God, Jesus, and us.

WHAT THE "I AM" SAYINGS TELL US ABOUT GOD

What is in a name? Have you ever thought about the meaning of your own name? For instance, my name, Rob, means "bright fame." Fuquay comes from a French word for "people." So Rob Fuquay means "famous person." When I tell my daughters that, they say, "In your dreams, Dad!"

So what does God's name tell us? Let's go back to the Exodus story. Why does Moses ask for God's name? God is calling Moses to a dangerous mission. Moses knows he will need some kind of evidence of just who this God is. Perhaps his Egyptian upbringing influenced him. Egyptians believed names possessed magical powers. Knowing one's name transferred some of the namesake's authority.

No wonder Moses wanted to know God's name! God was sending him to tell the most powerful man in the world what to do. Calling for the release of Hebrew slaves who were responsible for much of Egypt's prosperity sounded like lunacy. Moses had not been in Egypt since the day he fled for his life. Despite being a prince in Pharaoh's palace, Moses had killed an Egyptian soldier for beating a Hebrew slave. He was a wanted man. Now God tells him not only to return but to demand the release of God's people! Moses could lose his life. This expedition was more than risky; it was ridiculous. How could he know this mission stood any chance of success? He might not be the Prince of Egypt, but at least in Midian he was secure and comfortable.

If God was calling Moses to go, then he needed some reassurance. If he possessed some of the power of a God who could set a bush on fire without consuming it, then maybe he stood a chance. He probably remembered that in Egypt knowing a person's name gave you an advantage. He inquires of God, "If they ask me, 'What is his name?' what shall I say to them?"

This request comes in the midst of numerous excuses on Moses' part to get out of the assignment. Moses' protests include the following: "I am not respected . . . I am not eloquent . . . I am not brave . . . I don't even know your name!" To each of these, God replies, "I will be there." God does not say, "I'll make you feel important enough, or eloquent enough, or brave enough, or knowledgeable enough." Instead God simply says, "I will be there."

Everett Fox in his commentary on Exodus explains there is not a precise interpretation of God's name, which clarifies the mystery behind it. Some translate the word phrase, "I AM who I AM"; but Fox says others also interpret it to mean, "I will be there," so that what God is saying to Moses is, "I will be there howsoever I will be there."[1]

That interpretation gives new meaning to God's name. Moses desperately craves power and confidence. He seeks assurance that he will have what it takes to face this challenge, and God says, "I will be there. You need me more than power and ability. Let that be enough."

Moses has a decision to make. Will he wait to be faithful until God makes him feel adequate, or will he act faithfully and trust God's adequacy?

I heard a Christian comedian named Michael Jr. describe performing at a maximum security prison. He didn't go to the prison planning to do a show, but when the warden requested one, he felt a nudge from God to say yes.

Passing through the security scans, Michael thought, "Lord, I'm not prepared." He entered a room of rough-looking, expressionless men sitting in their prison jumpsuits. He kept thinking, "Now, Lord, would be a good time to give me something funny to say."

Michael walked toward the front of the group but still had nothing. His mind was blank. He stepped in front of the microphone. Right as his feet landed in the spot to perform he looked down at the front row. There sat a guy with a long white beard named Moses. He thought, "Thank you, Lord. I can do something with this!"

Michael said, who better to be in prison with than a guy named Moses? He pointed at the man and said, "Listen, I want you to go to the warden right now and say, "Let my people go!" The place erupted. It started an amazing routine of comedy that had the room howling. Michael Jr. said it was an experience unlike any he's ever had, and he learned a powerful lesson that day. He discovered that God would give him what he needed when his feet were where God wanted them to be.

The original ex-con named Moses had his feet where God wanted them to be that day on Sinai. God invited him to show up in Egypt. God's promise was simple, "You show up, and I will give you what you need. I will be there as I will be there. Let that be enough."

Have you ever wished God would do more to reassure you? Have you ever waited to act faithfully until feeling adequate? Have you ever delayed saying yes to a challenge because you were confident any number of people could do it better? Have you ever declined an opportunity because you were certain your skills weren't sufficient? Have you ever dodged an assignment because accepting would require you to grow?

Just remember, God's name is not "I Already Have." It is not "I Will Be." God's name is "I Am." It means God works in real time. God gives us what we need when our feet are where God wants them to be. God's promise is "I will be there as I will be there."

What the "I Am" Sayings Tell Us About Jesus

Now, let's jump to the New Testament. What do the "I Am" sayings tell us about Jesus? As mentioned earlier, by using these words Jesus identifies with the God of Moses. The God called "I Am" can be fully known in Jesus. Also, Jesus relates himself to very earthly things: bread, light, vine, shepherd, way.

At the same time, Jesus talks about these images in contrast to their opposites: bread versus hunger; light versus darkness; a good shepherd versus a hireling; a true vine versus a false one. In other words, Jesus is an answer for hunger, darkness, fear, emptiness, and so forth.

Gail R. O'Day, Dean and Professor of New Testament and Preaching at Wake Forest School of Divinity, says, "The 'I am' sayings . . . use symbols that come from the common fund of ancient Near Eastern religious and human experience. Through these common symbols, Jesus declares that people's religious needs and human longings are met in him."[2] Just as the Great I Am would be with Moses in his challenges, so Jesus vows to be with us in ours. In Jesus our greatest needs are met.

It's an old but beautiful story. A young boy walks into a pet shop to buy a puppy. The owner shows him what he has. The boy looks over each one carefully and finally makes his pick, one with a misshapen leg.

The owner says, "Son, you don't want that one. He can't even stand well. He'll never be able to run or fetch anything. Pick another."

The boy hikes up one pant leg revealing a prosthetic leg and replies, "Nope. This is the one for me. I know what it's like not to be able to run or play. I'll really be able to help him."

In Jesus we know a God willing to identify with our challenges. Jesus says, "I know what it's like to hurt. I know what it's like to receive news that a friend has died. I know what it's like to be betrayed by someone you love. I know what it's like to be treated unfairly. I know what it's like to be misunderstood. I know what it's like to suffer. I know what it's like to die. . . . I'll really be able to help them." For those who struggle, grieve, feel alone or rejected or afraid, Jesus says, I am able to satisfy, comfort, give meaning, and offer hope.

WHAT THE "I AM" SAYINGS TELL US ABOUT OURSELVES

Finally, the "I Am" sayings make claims about us:

- Jesus said, "I am the Light of the World" (John 8:12), but in another place: "*You* are the Light of the world" (Matt. 5:14, *emphasis added*).
- He said, "I am the Good Shepherd" (John 10:11) but also: "Feed my sheep" (John 21:17).
- He said, "I am the True Vine" (John 15:1) but as well: "You are the branches" (John 15:5).

- Jesus said, "I am the way, and the truth, and the life" (John 14:6), but later his followers were known as belonging to the Way (Acts 9:2).
- He said, "I am the Resurrection and the Life" (John 11:25) but equally promised us life abundant (John 10:10).

What each of these statements claims about God, it also claims about us. Together, they describe our nature and who we are.

Getting to know God means getting to know ourselves. The more we know who God is the more we know who we are.

Phillip Newell, the former Warden of the Iona Abbey in Scotland, spoke one morning in the church I serve. One of the statements he made really stuck with me: "We are not just made by God, we are made out of God." Think about that for a moment, and say it to yourself in the first person: "I am not just made by God, I am made out of God." It means we are made out of God's goodness, power, strength, and love.

Getting to know God means getting to know ourselves. The more we know who God is the more we know who we are.

Try this little exercise. Begin a statement with the words "I am. . . ." and finish it with six to ten characteristics that are true for you. What words do you use? Are you tempted to think first of your less desirable traits? "I am forgetful. I am out of shape. I am messy." Does it get worse? "I am hateful. I am prejudiced. I am addicted. I am ugly. I am hopeless."

If your first tendency is to think about what you wish were different about your life, then try another list. Write all the attributes you believe describe who God is. What does that include? Loving? Powerful? Forgiving? Beautiful? Creative? Compassionate? Gracious?

Remember, we are not just made *by* God, we are made *out of God*. Those attributes describe us too. Ultimately, they define us.

Who Are You? What Describes You?

Ash Wednesday marks the beginning of Lent. In churches everywhere people come forward to receive the sign of the cross smudged on their foreheads using ashes made of burned palm fronds from the previous Palm Sunday. Each year on Ash Wednesday I invite people to live with this question: "What do I have that cannot be reduced to ashes?" Just about everything in this life—our houses, our belongings, our clothes, and even our bodies—will all eventually be reduced to ashes. Yet God gives us something that cannot be destroyed. What part of you cannot be reduced to ashes? What word would describe it? That is who you really are.

What do I have that cannot be reduced to ashes?

I write these words after a visit to a woman in a hospice care center. She is a longtime member of my church who has battled cancer much of her life and recently learned it had returned. She probably has only a few days to live.

21

She was napping when I stopped by, but the family insisted I wake her because they knew she would want to see me. When she opened her eyes she smiled and said words she has spoken every time I have visited—literally every time! She said, "I am so blessed." With barely the energy to lift her arm or comb her hair she said, "I am so blessed." Sad that she wouldn't see her grandchildren graduate from high school she said, "I am so blessed." Wishing she had many more years to spend with the love of her life she said, "I am so blessed." About to depart this life she said, "I am. . . ." Her faith finished the sentence.

How does God help you finish your "I am. . . ."?

Reflection/Discussion Questions

Do you know what your name means (both first and last)? If not, try researching it and see if you think your name truly fits!

Why was knowing God's name so important to Moses?

What do you think is significant about God's name in Exodus 3:14? What message is God sending Moses by telling God's name?

Based on the example of Moses, what can we learn today about carrying out tough assignments from God?

Thinking about Jesus' use of the words I Am, *what does it mean that Jesus associates himself with symbols like bread, light, shepherding, a grapevine, a way, and so forth?*

What does the statement "We are not just made by God, we are made out of God" mean to you?

How do you end a sentence that begins, "I am. . . ."?

Note that a page is included in each chapter so you can write answers to these questions or make notes for your group meeting, if you are participating in a group study.

NOTES

_____
_____
_____
_____
_____
_____
_____
_____
_____
_____
_____
_____
_____
_____
_____
_____
_____
_____
_____
_____

2

"I Am the Bread of Life"
Knowing God's Satisfaction

John 6:27-59

There is a difference between being full and being satisfied.

Have you ever had this experience? I was ready to go to bed one night but felt a little hungry. I wanted something to eat before calling it a night, but what would satisfy? I stared into the refrigerator. It was full of food, but nothing was appealing. I tried a piece of leftover chicken from supper the night before. It looked better than it tasted. I heated up a few bites of casserole. Again, same result. Maybe something sweet? I ate a little ice cream. That tasted better, but I still wanted something more. I finally went to bed feeling full, just not satisfied.

Being full and being satisfied aren't the same, yet we live in a world that would have us think they are. We are tempted to believe that in order to be satisfied we have to be full, yet fullness does not guarantee satisfaction in many areas of our lives. Someone asked J. D. Rockefeller how much money was enough? He responded, "Just a little bit more." Fullness does not guarantee satisfaction.

Let's think about the varieties of fullness in our world. There is fullness of noise. Walk in any store or restaurant and you get sensory overload: multiple television screens each tuned to different programs while background music blares through speakers. I read my own words here and admit I sound hypocritical. I watch my share of television and seldom go without the radio on when I'm in the car. Am I afraid of silence?

We are full of communications. Few people are more than a step away from devices that keep them in touch with everyone they know. Some are never even a step away! My three teenage daughters have learned to navigate multiple conversations at one time. While I am talking with them, they are texting someone else on the phone and communicating with yet another on the computer through Facebook or Instagram. When I ask how they keep all those conversations going at the same time, they look at me as if I have two heads. For me it would take two heads to manage it all. I can't follow a conversation with myself sometimes.

We are full of—*stuff*! How's that for a technical word? But what word captures it better? How much stuff do you have? When I moved to college I could carry all my worldly possessions in the backseat of my Toyota Celica. When I moved to seminary I needed the trunk as well. When I moved to my first parsonage I needed a pickup truck. (It didn't require more because the parsonage was furnished!) When I got married and we moved to our second appointment, we needed a U-Haul.

When my wife and I had children and were being assigned to another church, my dad offered to help us move. We went to pick out the truck.

He convinced me the smaller size would be adequate, and besides, it would save quite a bit of money. I wasn't sure but deferred to his experience. Church members helped us load the truck on a 100-degree day. We packed every square inch of the truck and saw a sofa, tables, chairs, and a couple dozen boxes still sitting in the driveway with storm clouds looming. With incredible humility and ownership of the situation, my dad said, "Son, you've just got too much stuff." Profound!

Do you ever look at the stuff in your closets, basement, or attic and ask, "Where did all this come from?" Chances are it wasn't just the store. Deep inside we can be driven by a need for more. Sometimes we are driven by a fear of letting go of what we have. Our society coined the phrase "shopping therapy." We now have support groups for hoarders. A subtle message is whispered into our spirits telling us that fullness equals satisfaction. But we know that's not true.

Deep inside we can be driven by a need for more.

When my girls were little they loved watching *Veggie Tales* videos. One was a particular favorite: Madame Blueberry. The story is about a very wealthy blueberry who lives in a tree house filled with all the stuff she ever wanted. She thought having more stuff would make her happy, yet happiness was always out of reach. Therefore she was always blue (yeah, I know). Every day she sang the same little song that began, "I'm so blue, I don't know what to do." That's what the drive for fullness does. It can turn you blue!

How can you tell if you are driven by a need for fullness? Just ask yourself this question: What can I not live without? Is there anything? Do you find yourself needing to eat until you feel full? What if your cell phone or Internet went down? How do you react when the cable television is out? What if you had to get rid of half your possessions? What things do you feel you couldn't live without? You may be driven by a need for fullness. If so, then satisfaction in life becomes a conditional quality. If so, then know this: You aren't the first to feel this way.

SEEKING FULLNESS IN JESUS' DAY

The drive to feel full characterized society in Jesus' day also. That is the backstory to this first saying, "I am the Bread of Life." Jesus spoke these words in response to a crowd that followed him around the Sea of Galilee. The day before, Jesus had performed a miracle by feeding thousands of hungry people by multiplying protein and carbohydrates—otherwise known as fish and loaves.

Jesus said to them, "I am the bread of life. Whoever comes to me will never be hungry, and whoever believes in me will never be thirsty."

JOHN 6:35

This is the only miracle story, except for the Resurrection, told in all four Gospels. Matthew, Mark and Luke report that after everyone finished eating they were "satisfied" (Matthew 14:20; Mark 6:42; Luke

9:17). John, however, says they all ate "and were full" (6:26). They were full but it doesn't say they were satisfied. The next day they went looking for Jesus, who had gone to the lakeside village of Capernaum.

That's the problem with chasing fullness. There is never enough.

You would think Jesus would be encouraged by thousands of people searching for him, but he knew why they came. They were just looking for another miracle. They were driven by a need for fullness. Therefore Jesus told them that he could give something lasting and complete. In response, the crowd asked him, "What sign are you going to give us then, so that we may see it and believe you?" (John 6:30). Think about that response for a moment. The crowd is fewer than twenty-four hours removed from a miracle and they are asking, "What can you do for us now?" That's the problem with chasing fullness. There is never enough. We always need more. It keeps us on the lookout for the next miracle.

Not only that, a drive for fullness makes it hard to enjoy what we have. This is the insidious nature of hunger. It makes us consumers more than enjoyers! Yet the moment we buy, we experience a letdown because it's the need for more that propels us. Golfers provide a good example. The worst thing a golfer can do is swing someone else's club. A better score is now just a purchase away.

The crowd asked Jesus, "What work are you performing? Our ancestors ate the manna in the wilderness; as it is written, 'He gave them bread from heaven to eat'" (6:30-31). They were referring to the forty-year period in Israel's history when the people wandered in the wilderness. Following the exodus from Egypt they journeyed through the Sinai Peninsula before entering the Promised Land. They gave up their slave rations for freedom, but once in the desert they were hungry, so God provided a miracle. Every day they received manna, bread from heaven. All they had to do was go out each morning and collect it. No long searches. No cooking or baking required. There was just one caveat: They could gather only what they needed for that day. They couldn't hoard it. There were no support groups in the wilderness. They couldn't stockpile their blessings, but they could live with the satisfaction of knowing God would take care of them . . . every day . . . one day at a time.

Standing by the Sea of Galilee in Capernaum the crowd reminded Jesus of this. Why? Perhaps they wanted a miracle that would take away any worries from life. If Jesus really was connected to the Great I Am, then maybe he could provide assurance that God would take care of tomorrow's problems.

Have you ever put those kinds of conditions on God? Have you ever thought, *If I attend worship regularly, do some good deeds for others, and give some money to the church or charity, then it ought to merit something.* Have you ever felt that a by-product of your faith should be a satisfaction that doesn't require much work?

Jesus replied to the crowd, "Very truly, I tell you, . . . my Father who gives you the true bread from heaven. . . . gives life to the world."

"Sir," they said, "give us this bread always" (6:32-34). Do you feel a sense of desperation there? "Give us . . . always." They were saying, "Don't let us go to bed tonight without knowing we will have what we need in the morning." It's easy to turn faith into a lifetime Certificate of Deposit, to want some guarantee that our interests will be covered. For people looking for a CD kind of faith, Jesus declared, "I am the bread of life" (6:35). Jesus is offering satisfaction, but the people are chasing fullness.

In an article for *Discipleship Journal*, Jean Zornes relates this Bible story to her life. She says that she assumed that Jesus' job was taking care of all her needs and wants—jobs, roommates, a husband, and so on.

> But after a while my tastes got fussier. . . . When those things didn't come, I felt as if Jesus had walked away from me. What I didn't realize was that He had put loving distance between us, just as He did with the crowd (by the sea that day).[1]

Can you relate? Have you ever said to God, "If you'll just give me 'this,' I'll be so happy," only to find out that the happiness expiration date on "this" was pretty short? When life becomes just a matter of chasing fullness, happiness is always temporary. There is always another need, another want, another crisis, another something that keeps us from being satisfied.

Practices of Satisfaction

C. S. Lewis said, "I sometimes wonder whether all pleasures are not substitutes for joy."[2] In saying "I am the Bread of Life," Jesus is in effect telling us, "I don't want you to spend your life just chasing fullness. I want to offer satisfaction, no matter what the circumstances are. I want to give you contentment and peace. I can provide that. Let me be your source of joy, so that no matter where you are, you can say, 'Right now is a good day. Life is good. I am blessed.'"

C. S. Lewis said, "I sometimes wonder whether all pleasures are not substitutes for joy."

How can we get to that place? How can we discover Jesus as a source of satisfaction? Let me offer a few practices. I'm sure the first one will excite you!

Fasting

Normally we associate fasting with food, such as skipping a meal or going a day without eating. That is fasting, to be sure, but let's expand the concept. Fasting can include breaking from any routine or pattern for a given amount of time. It could mean fasting from food in general or some specific foods we have come to depend on: coffee, alcohol, bread, desserts, sugar, and so forth.

Fasting might include technology, such as turning off computers and cell phones for certain hours of the day—preferably waking ones! It could also include fasting from unnecessary spending or setting a goal to save a certain amount of money each week.

If you wonder what would be your most beneficial fast, just ask yourself what is hardest to go without. Fasting from that could be a helpful way of focusing on Christ as a source of satisfaction.

Every Lent, when I talk about fasting, some jokester will say something like, "I'm fasting from exercise and eating spinach." Sorry, that doesn't count. The point is to fast from habits that have the potential for unhealthy control over us. Why do this? There are several reasons.

The discomfort of going without something we enjoy is meant to be a routine way of recalling the suffering of Christ on our behalf. It is a like a string around our spiritual thumbs reminding us of what Christ did for us.

John Wesley, founder of the Methodist movement, used to fast from food twice a week because of the way it opened him to the power of God. It was such an important practice that for a time he wouldn't ordain people unless they committed to fasting.

We also fast as a way of making room for other things. In skipping a meal we make time to pray or serve. In shutting off technology we are more available to family and friends. In reducing spending we have more to give away. We fast as a way of practicing self-denial. We deny ourselves so that our appetites don't consume us. When we can say no, we give our spirits authority over our bodies instead of the other way around.

Move from Expecting to Accepting

Another way to know satisfaction is to learn to accept what God puts in front of us each day. When I was growing up, my parents were not real big on giving choices as to what we ate at meals. They taught my siblings and me that you ate what was put before you and you were grateful for it. Every now and then my mother in a moment of weakness would ask, "I don't know what to cook tonight, what do you kids want?" But before we could answer, she would catch herself and say, "Never mind, I'll figure it out."

I didn't appreciate the lesson at the time, and I don't know that my parents did it for some life value—they just didn't want to hear a lot of complaining—but I came to find tremendous spiritual purpose in this little practice. I learned that choosiness doesn't lead to happiness. I am tempted at times to believe that having full choice and placing my happiness at the center will bring satisfaction.

If you disagree, then make your personal happiness Job One for a while and ask yourself the Dr. Phil question: "How's that working for you?" Being in control might bring tastes of satisfaction but not the lasting kind.

In my prayers I frequently like to tell God what I want. I begin my day with list in hand: "Today, God, I need answers for this problem; I need resources for this issue; I need you to clear up this situation, change this person, resolve this crisis," and so on. Sometimes I even slip and call God "Santa."

Real satisfaction comes, however, when I pray differently. "Lord, thank you for what is set before me today. Help me to recognize and enjoy the special blessings you will offer me. I am going to choose to be thankful." Another way of looking at this is to make being satisfied of higher importance than getting full. You see, getting full is something we can control. We are in charge of choosing. We can do the things that will fill life up, but satisfaction is something we need help with. We sometimes need assistance from God in order to say, "I have the gifts and opportunity to be satisfied right now. I already possess what is necessary for joy."

What does it mean to believe that satisfaction is available each day? Try this as a personal experiment. Each morning as you wake up, pretend it's Christmas Day. Remember as a child waking up on Christmas morning with an excitement that made you feel like you were about to burst? Why did you have that? Because you knew gifts were waiting to be discovered. How might it change you to begin each day believing that? We often wake up feeling the opposite, that it's just another day. It's another day of school or work or routine. We think we know what awaits us. We are focused on the less exciting parts of our day and assume those experiences will define it. Amazing how easy it is to realize low expectations.

Try believing that good gifts await you, things you can't see or predict. Treat each day as Christmas, remembering that people, food, home, work, school are all God's gifts to you. What if you treated them like manna—God's blessings to be enjoyed that day? Would it build your trust in God to satisfy your needs?

Focus More on Feeding Than on Being Fed

Finally, one more practice of satisfaction: Focus on making others full instead of making yourself full. Jesus said, "I am the Bread of Life." He also made it clear that following him meant taking up a cross. Dining with Jesus can give you splinters. Seeking to live a redemptive life is not just about what we do for others. It is about what doing for others can do for us. Making an effort for others provides a satisfaction that can't be found when fullness is all we seek.

I recently read an inspiring story about making an effort for others. The story comes from an episode of the show called *Chopped* on Food Network. What better way to close a chapter about bread?

Contestants on *Chopped* are usually chefs and professional cooks who compete for a nice cash prize and the honor of being "*Chopped* Champion." They have limited time to prepare a gourmet meal with odd foods and ingredients. In one episode it came down to a cook-off between Lance Nitahara, a chef at a resort in the Adirondacks, and a French woman living in the United States named Yoanne Magris.

She wanted to win so she could fly back to France and visit her dying grandmother.

During one of the interviews, Lance talked about his faith. Lance said, "Before God, I was a jerk. I was okay with stepping over people if I wanted. But now, I'm able to do things with grace."

In the final round on the show, Nitahara edged Magris out. Yoanne got "chopped." As she started to walk away, Nitahara said, "Wait. I didn't expect to win, so I wasn't expecting any money from this. You deserved to win as much as I did, and you deserve to see your grandmother, so I'm going to give you the ticket."

People were stunned. No one had ever given away the prize money like that. Lance said, "What I've discovered from my faith is that it's not about the destination but the journey, and today the journey was great."[3]

We discover the value of the journey when we make Christ our sustenance. When Jesus is my bread of life, I can let go of that need to get all I can for myself and have life my way. I am free to give and share and enjoy. I can say to God, "Lord, you've already given me what I need for satisfaction, so I'm just going to enjoy it and look for ways to share it."

Are you satisfied—or just trying to get full? How does your satisfaction overflow into giving to others?

Reflection/Discussion Questions

How do you relate to the idea of "chasing after fullness"?

List all the types of fullness you can identify in our world. Now write down your personal definition of satisfaction. *How many items in the previous list can provide satisfaction for you?*

Thinking about the people in John 6 who followed Jesus looking for another miracle, what similarities do you see today in the way people follow Jesus?

If the people in this story represent all of humanity, what does it say about us that we can receive a miracle one day and on the next say to God, "What will you do for us now?"

How do you understand C. S. Lewis's words, "I sometimes wonder whether all pleasures are substitutes for joy"?

Given the context of the story, what do you think Jesus meant when he said, "I am the Bread of Life"?

What does it mean to go from expecting to accepting?

Have you ever experienced a sense of being fed when you focused on feeding others?

NOTES

_____

_____

_____

_____

_____

_____

_____

_____

_____

_____

_____

_____

_____

_____

_____

_____

_____

_____

_____

_____

_____

3

"I Am the Light of the World"
Knowing God's Guidance

John 7:2, 14; 8:12

The words *I Am* have an eternal quality about them. If you are named "I Am," it means you always have been and always will be. When Jesus says, "I Am," it means he is accessible for all eternity. Space and time do not limit our ability to encounter Jesus.

Tony Campolo illustrates this concept using Einstein's theory of relativity. According to Einstein, time is relative to motion. The faster we travel the more time is compressed. If you were put into a rocket ship and sent to outer space traveling at the speed of 170,000 miles per second and returned after ten years, how much older would you be? It's a trick question. You would be ten years older. However, everyone else would be twenty years older! The faster you travel the more time is compressed. If you traveled at 180,000 miles per second, twenty years would be compressed into one day. Pretty amazing, isn't it?

Tony Campolo explains that you can't travel at the speed of light because as you approach that speed your physical mass expands in weight and size. He says, "Don't ever let anyone say you are fat—just tell them that you are traveling too fast!"[1] Yet, if we could travel at the speed of light, there would be no passage of time at all. All of time would be compressed into one eternal moment.

Now that will blow your mind, won't it?

Maybe that is why Jesus could say, "Before Abraham was, I am" (John 8:58). He is the light of the world. All of time gets compressed in him. We can encounter eternity in Jesus.

You could say the story of the Bible is one of moving from darkness to light.

Light is an important theme in the Bible. You could say the story of the Bible is one of moving from darkness to light. Look at the way the Bible begins in Genesis: "The earth was a formless void and darkness covered the face of the deep . . . Then God said, "Let there be light"; and there was light" (1:2-3). The first thing God spoke into existence was light.

Go to the book of Revelation, to the description of the new heaven and earth: "There will be no more night; they need no light of lamp or sun, for the Lord God will be their light" (22:5). Many of the prophecies of a coming messiah use the image of light: "Arise, shine; for your light has come" (Isa. 60:1). "The people who walked in darkness have seen a great light" (Isa. 9:2). The Bible constantly affirms that when God comes on the scene, there is light. God makes darkness a choice. With that in mind, let's look closer at Jesus' words, "I am the Light of the World" and two contexts that surround them.

ALWAYS ON A JOURNEY

The first context is historical. In the opening of John 7 we learn that Jesus was attending the Feast of Tabernacles, also known as the Feast of Booths. It was celebrated in the fall to commemorate the Israelites' journey through the wilderness after leaving Egypt. Note that this is another "I Am" saying connected with the wilderness experience in Israel's history.

Each year, the people were to build booths, or as they are called in Hebrew, *sukkots* (pronounced "sue-coats"). The name may come from the first town where the Hebrews stayed after leaving Egypt (Exod. 12:37). During the wilderness years, people lived in temporary shelters that could easily be set up and taken down since they were frequently on the move.

Again Jesus spoke to them, saying, "I am the light of the world. Whoever follows me will never walk in darkness but will have the light of life."

JOHN 8:12

Moses instructed them that when they left the wilderness and entered the Promised Land, they were to remember this experience. Every year the Hebrews were to keep a Festival of Booths, or Tabernacles, and live in *sukkots* for seven days (see Deuteronomy 16:13-15). This is still practiced today. Every Jewish family is to build a *sukkah* and eat meals in it as a way of observing the festival. I was able to visit Jerusalem recently and saw for myself the colorful way that this festival is still experienced by the Jewish people.

What is the significance? The practice is a reminder that life is a pilgrimage. When the Jews had to dwell in *sukkots* in the wilderness, it was clear this was temporary. They were headed to a Promised Land where one day they would build more lasting homes. No more shelters. No more roaming. No more manna and quail. They would become farmers and landowners and builders. They would take care of themselves. They would be able to say, "We have arrived!"

Arrival is a myth! We never fully arrive in this life.

Perhaps this is why God told them to keep this festival as a perpetual practice. Arrival is a myth! We never fully arrive in this life. Even when the Israelites reached the Promised Land, God wanted them to understand they would still be on a journey. This world is not their final destination. They kept this annual tradition as a way of remembering life is a pilgrimage. Our ultimate Promised Land is beyond this world.

The Ultimate Destination

Think for a moment about what it means to believe that life is a pilgrimage and everything in this world is just temporary. When I understand and accept that, I realize I never fully get "there." When I become frustrated with where I am and begin asking, "When will I ever get there?" I have to remember, never! At least not in this life. My ultimate destination is to be with God. My "there" is beyond any destination of this world. God determines my "there." So the next time someone says to you, "You're not all there," just smile and say, "Not yet, anyway!"

This belief that life is a journey is liberating. When you find yourself in an unwanted place, you can know that place is not a destination. It's just a stopping point. Have you been thankful that some places in your life were just stopping points?

Some would say that hell is the ultimate stopping point—an eternal unwanted destination. In the Old Testament the word for hell is *sheol*. It means "place of darkness." In a really dark place you don't see a future. But when you know that life is a journey, it keeps stopping places from becoming staying places!

Just Passing Through

I once worked with a church lay leader who had an annoying habit: He was perpetually positive. He wasn't just happy or encouraging. He saw a bright spot no matter what, even when I didn't always want to see one.

When I shared some tale of woe about matters in the church, he would listen and softly reply, "Ain't it gonna be wonderful to see how the Lord works through all this?" It wasn't so much a question as a declaration. Count on it every time. No matter how bad the tale, "Ain't it gonna be wonderful. . . ."At times I could have gagged him! There's positive, and then there's Pollyanna. I wanted someone who would climb down in the pit with me and agree that it's dark and awful, rather than tell me how bright it is at the top. This man, however, didn't linger long in unwanted places.

One day I got a call that his wife had received a diagnosis of terminal cancer. She had only a few months to live. I raced over to the house. After a lengthy visit we prayed together. There was no avoidance of reality. There was clear recognition of what this diagnosis meant. He walked me to the car. Before I got in, he turned to hug me and with tears rolling down his face said, "Ain't it gonna be wonderful to see how the Lord works through all this?"

This true journeyman of faith lived as a pilgrim. He didn't deny life's challenges. He understood that no place in this life is permanent. We just have stopping places, not staying places.

SIGNS ALONG THE WAY

How did the Israelites know that their stopping places in the wilderness were not staying places? They had two pillars they could always see that confirmed God's presence: a pillar of cloud by day and a pillar of fire by night (Exod. 13:21). The whole time they were in the wilderness, they could see those pillars. They knew it was time to move when the pillar started moving. Their journey was following God.

Of course, when the Israelites reached the Promised Land, the pillars disappeared. They could have thought they had arrived, that now they didn't have to depend on God's guidance anymore. But that wasn't the case. God wanted them to seek God's guidance in a deeper way. God gave them the Festival of Tabernacles to remember they still needed God's guidance. It is God who keeps stopping places from becoming staying places.

For us, the significance of understanding this reality is not just to realize we are always on a journey but to ask, "God, where do you want to lead me?"

The Feast of Tabernacles was the context in which Jesus said, "I am the light of the world." Most likely he said it on a special night during the Feast of Tabernacles called the Grand Illumination. Giant torches lining the courtyard of the temple burned so brightly that all of Jerusalem was illuminated. The wicks were made from . . . are you ready for this? . . . the worn-out undergarments of the priests. That's right, priests' old underwear is what they used to light the giant torches. I can imagine there are a few denominational leaders who would like to reinstate this practice, just to know they could light a fire under some preachers!

The night of Grand Illumination, the opening of the Festival of Tabernacles, was a huge celebration. People would sing and dance until morning light. In that context Jesus said, "I am the Light of the World." Jesus was saying, "For those who understand life is a journey, for those who seek light and direction through all of life's stopping places, I will be your pillar."

What does that truth look like in our everyday living? What does it mean to trust Christ as a source of light in our world?

FLASHLIGHT FAITH

Think about how a flashlight works. Let's say you are camping and need to go the restroom after dark. It is a little distance from your site, so you take a flashlight. You are too far away for the light to illuminate the location of the facility. All the flashlight can do is illuminate the next few steps. The point of a flashlight is not to show you the destination but the next steps.

When you trust Christ as a source of light, he gives direction one step at a time. This can be frustrating, especially if you need to know where your steps will take you. However, if life is a journey and not a destination, then Christ determines "there." It makes things easier. You don't have to worry about where you'll end up. You can focus on following directions.

Maybe that direction will be to take a step of reconciliation in a relationship. That may be an intimidating prospect. What if the other person is not receptive? What if your action makes things worse? We can't know. We can't see the end of the path, just the next steps.

We need God more than the courage we want from God.

Maybe that direction will be to take a step of honesty and speak the truth. Such steps can be painful, risking a friendship or even a job. Decisions like this need to be carefully considered, but instead of needing God to show where such steps will lead, you just ask God to show which next step is the right one.

Maybe that direction will be to take a step toward a dream or goal. Fear of failure may hold you back. You wait to take a step until you can see the chance for success. In the meantime you stand still. But such steps require a flashlight kind of faith, trusting a step at a time. It takes a lot of steps in the wilderness to reach the Promised Land.

Remember the interpretation of God's words to Moses, "I will be there howsoever I will be there." We need God more than the courage we want from God.

The next time you face a challenge or difficult decision for which you seek God's guidance, try this. Every morning get up twenty or thirty minutes earlier than normal. Go to a quiet place where you can be alone. Light a candle. Quiet yourself before God for a few minutes and then thank God for being present with you, as symbolized by that light. Then give thanks for blessings in your life. This practice builds confidence that no matter what the challenge you face, there are still blessings to celebrate. Now, make your request known. State your challenge and what you need. After that ask, "Dear Lord, how can I honor you in this situation?" Pause. Be still. See what comes to you. Don't process the thoughts. Don't contend with how you will carry out any idea that comes or what that idea might require. Just let the thoughts come. Write them down. Keep a pad and pencil nearby.

Do this over several days and see what repeating themes or actions emerge. Once you sense some direction, ask God to show you the next step. Don't make seeing the end of the path the goal, just knowing the next step.

OPEN TO NEW UNDERSTANDING

To this point we have considered Jesus' words in the historical context, but there was another important context surrounding that night. It was a night not only of celebration but also of great tension.

At the beginning of John 7, along with learning it was the Feast of Tabernacles, we also discover that the Sanhedrin were meeting. This council of religious leaders met in a place called the Hall of Hewn Stones built in the north wall of the Temple mount. They gathered daily to consider religious affairs except on the sabbath and during festivals. So why were they meeting during the Feast of Tabernacles? They were moving quickly to put Jesus to death. They sent guards to arrest him, but unfortunately for the council, the guards were mesmerized by Jesus' teaching. They reported, "Never has anyone spoken like this!" (7:46). The leaders accused the guards of being deceived like the rest of the crowds listening to Jesus.

It was in that gathering of religious leaders that Nicodemus spoke up on behalf of Jesus. We first heard of Nicodemus earlier in the book of John when he went to see Jesus alone. It was also at night, in the darkness. Remember that when God comes on the scene, there is light.

Nicodemus was struggling to come to a new understanding of God because of Jesus. His old ideas were being challenged. There is no way to know exactly how Nicodemus' opinions changed that night, but now he was standing up for Jesus among peers who wanted to have Jesus put to death.

This represents one of the most courageous movements in the spiritual life—the willingness to be open to a new idea, a new revelation. To say that something you once held sacred, something that was very important, might not be right. To have the courage to say, "Perhaps I have more to learn or understand. Maybe God has further insight to offer me about some matter I once felt very clear about."

While all of this was going on inside the buildings of the Temple, outside Jesus was saying, "I am the Light of the World." In Jesus there is truth. When we let him be our light, he exposes what needs to change or be brought to a newer understanding. Letting that happen takes courage.

When I was growing up I would often spend a week or two in the summers at my grandmother's house in Durham, North Carolina. She lived one block from the Durham Bulls' baseball park in an old Victorian home. She loved my visits because she loved me—and because she got free labor. My job was washing windows. My grandmother would give me clear (yes, pun intended!) instructions on how to clean the windows so I didn't leave streaks across the pane or grime in the corners.

When I started to work in the morning she would leave me with these words, "I'll be back in the afternoon to check." I would think to myself, *Afternoon! Are you crazy? It won't take nearly that long. Come back in thirty minutes.*

Afternoon would arrive and she would call me to go with her to inspect my work. That inspection felt like the Final Judgment. She would ask if I washed the windows like she told me. I always felt like that was one last chance to come clean (yes, another pun). Then she would pull back the curtain. Organ music or something should have swelled in the background. Before me was the result of my life's deeds . . . or at least that morning's. Streaky windows and dirty corners stood out. But how? I didn't see them in the morning. Everything looked fine. How did they get there? What enemy had done this?

Of course, no one did anything to the windows. My grandmother knew that the afternoon sunlight would reveal the truth of their condition. I discovered something very important: stick to vacuuming!

The closer I stay to Jesus the more I allow his truth to search me like the afternoon sun. Sometimes it reveals unpleasant and difficult areas of my life. Sometimes it brings me to a new understanding about positions I once felt were airtight. No matter how challenging, Jesus' light always brings me to a better place.

When George Wallace was governor of Alabama in the 1960s, he was the face and voice of segregation and racism in the South. He blocked the entrance to the University of Alabama so black students couldn't enter. He directed state troopers to use billy clubs on non-violent protestors, including children. He did this while professing to be a good Christian man. His famous slogan was, "Segregation now, segregation tomorrow, segregation forever."

The closer I stay to Jesus, the more
I allow his truth to search me like
the afternoon sun.

But later in his life something changed George Wallace. A would-be assassin's bullet left him paralyzed. He went through significant suffering. He felt God use that suffering to bring understanding to the plight of the black population on whom he had inflicted so much hardship. He changed. He realized he was wrong and found a way out of his darkness. The light of Jesus Christ met him. He felt Christ say, "I can restore you to joy, but something has to be removed in your heart." His son stated in an interview that his father's suffering helped him to understand the suffering of others.[2]

Sometimes the journey to greater joy and liberation is a difficult one. It takes us through a wilderness of sorts. Yet, as long as we stay on the journey, we refuse to let stopping places become staying places, and we experience darkness being turned to light.

Our darkness is not always of our own making. Sometimes our paths are just cloudy. We can't see the destination. We don't know how the road will end. All we can do is trust Christ one step at a time.

Sometimes our darkness is a result of our own actions. When we come to such acknowledgments, as painful as they are, we can know that being able to admit our fault is a result of Christ working within us. We have not been abandoned. We are not beyond grace. Part of the work of Christ's light is to reveal truth, not to condemn us but to spare us (John 3:17).

That's what Nicodemus heard that first night he met Jesus. Maybe that's why he stood up for Jesus on the same night Jesus said, "I am the Light of the World." Maybe that's why Nicodemus provided the burial spices to anoint Jesus' body after he was crucified, taking one last chance to honor him . . . in the light of day.

Reflection/Discussion Questions

If the significance of light as a metaphor in the Bible shows how God makes darkness a choice, can you relate to ways God gave you choice over some kind of darkness?

When was a time in your life that you were grateful that a "stopping place" was not a "staying place"?

Can you think of a time when the flashlight illustration would have been a good one to describe your faith?

Knowing that Jesus spoke these words at the Feast of Booths, what do you think he meant when he said, "I am the Light of the World"? What do you think his listeners understood when he said those words?

We sometimes hear people use the expression, "he (or she) is in a dark place." What do people typically mean? Think about the religious leaders plotting to kill Jesus. How did darkness work there?

How have you experienced Jesus as a source of light in a time of darkness?

"Light of the World" is one metaphor Jesus uses for himself and us. What does it mean for us to be a light for the world?

Notes

_____

_____

_____

_____

_____

_____

_____

_____

_____

_____

_____

_____

_____

_____

_____

_____

_____

_____

_____

_____

NOTES

_____
_____
_____
_____
_____
_____
_____
_____
_____
_____
_____
_____
_____
_____
_____
_____
_____
_____
_____
_____
_____

4

"I Am the Good Shepherd"
Knowing God's Care

John 10:1-10

In this chapter we look at two of Jesus' "I Am" sayings: "I am the Good Shepherd," and "I am the Gate (or Door) for the sheep." These sayings reveal much about God's care for us. Typically sheep pens in Jesus' day were a configuration of tall rock walls with only one entrance. Sheep spent their lives traveling in and out of doorways. They came in through the gate for security and rest. Inside the pen they were free from predators or bandits. A good shepherd who cared about the condition of his flock would often inspect each sheep as it entered through the gate. The shepherd would look for parasites or injuries and properly tend to them. The gate represented security.

Sheep also went out through the gates to find pasture and enjoyment. In the pasture sheep could roam, run, and feel alive. If you haven't noticed before, sheep enjoy grazing. The gate led to joy.

A good shepherd always watched over the sheep coming in and going out. Once again we can see why the Bible compares people to sheep. We all spend our lives traveling through a similar doorway. Every one one of us is constantly moving between a search for familiarity and a return to security.

If you think I overstate the case, consider a few questions. Do you sit in or near the same place in church every Sunday? Do you frequent a Starbucks or restaurant where a server can predict your order? At Christmas and birthdays do you get more than three gifts of the same type? Most of us have well-worn paths leading to familiarity and security.

On the other hand, what about our search for "pastures," places of excitement and enjoyment? Here are a few questions to think about. Have you in the last month spent time daydreaming or thinking about plans for a vacation or getaway? Have you spent time in the last month working on or thinking about a different job you would like to have? Or a different house? Sometimes, what feels like security starts to become a prison.

Like sheep we regularly come in and go out. Think of that pattern as an analogy for life. All of us are moving through that space all the time. We are in constant flow between our search for familiarity and predictability and at the same time seeking newness, excitement, and a break from our routines.

The psalmist said, "The LORD will keep your going out and your coming in from this time on and forevermore" (121:8). Many passages in the Bible speak of our coming in and going out. God knows our need for joy, abundance, and feeling alive as well as our need for security, comfort, and protection.

Jesus calls himself a Good Shepherd because he provides security and comfort in the lives of those who seek to live under his care. His very life serves as a doorway. Let's understand a little more about what's behind this image.

In John 10 we find two different images of Jesus, depending on the translation. Some translations use *gate* while others use *door*. Both images convey important understandings about God's care.

JESUS AS THE GATE

Let's consider the first image: the sheep gate. These gates were used for sheep pens often built alongside buildings in a town or village. The pens would have a sturdy structure with tall walls and a completely enclosed locking door or gate. These types of enclosures might be owned or managed by a shepherd; but more often than not, they were rented. Either way, a shepherd would pay to keep the sheep in this kind of pen. Sometimes an owner would have a watchman who kept the keys and opened the gate for those shepherds who paid rent.

If people didn't enter through the gate, they had to climb over the wall, which most likely meant they were thieves. That didn't mean they wanted to hurt the sheep. They just wanted to steal them. Hurting the sheep would be the last thing thieves would do. They would need the sheep to be in good condition so they could sell them. They simply used sheep for their own gain or advantage.

Have you ever known people like that? They weren't out to cause you harm, but they didn't really care about your well-being—they cared about what you could do for them. Maybe they wanted to be around you because of your generosity. They knew you were a gracious person, so the only time you heard from them was when they had something to ask.

Maybe you have a serving nature. You gladly help others in need no matter what the tasks, but over time you realize that certain "friends" seek you most when they are in a crisis.

Maybe you are popular. Perhaps you are successful or hold a significant position. People seek you out because it makes them feel better about themselves to be associated with you. They mean you no harm, but you wonder if they would still seek you if your position changed.

So again Jesus said to them, "Very truly, I tell you, I am the gate for the sheep. All who came before me are thieves and bandits; but the sheep did not listen to them. I am the gate. Whoever enters by me will be saved, and will come in and go out and find pasture."

JOHN 10:7-9

In seminary I took several classes under retired bishop Nolan Harmon who was nearing one hundred at the time. Someone asked him one day how it felt when he retired from the episcopacy. He said, "When I was a bishop it was like being a stagecoach driver" (appropriate analogy since he lived in the era of stagecoaches). "I had the reins in my hand. They were attached to a powerful team of horses, and all kinds of folks were in the carriage. Then I retired. I really didn't feel like anything changed. I still had the reins in my hand, but when I looked up I saw they weren't attached to any horses! And, of course, everyone got out of the coach!"

People seek out other people for all kinds of reasons. It doesn't mean they are out to harm them. It just means their own interests blur the well-being of those they seek. You can usually tell when someone's interest is genuine.

On February 17, 2013, the country music world was shocked by the death of Mindy McCready. She was a beautiful young woman who rose to stardom in the 1990s, but maintaining that stardom was difficult. She struggled with addictions. She tried to take her life on several occasions, eventually succeeding.

In the weeks following her death a number of revelations about her life emerged. Someone said that her worst addiction was men. As beautiful as she was, she would seek men who would make her feel valued and special. Unfortunately many of these men just took advantage of her.

When she was fifteen years old, Mindy had an affair with a well-known professional baseball player. A string of relationships followed. Over time her life spiraled downward until she finally met a man she felt genuinely loved her for who she was. It was a temporary turnaround until he left her. He killed himself. About a month after his suicide, she went to the place where he took his life, and she took her own.

In so many ways Mindy McCready had everything going for her. Though beautiful and talented, her self-image was deeply tied to others' opinions. People gladly showed interest in her as long as she was famous. She had people climbing the walls to get to her.

Deep inside of every human heart is a desire to be loved. We want to know we matter and that someone genuinely cares about us. Jesus said, "I am the Good Shepherd" because he comes through the gate. He's paid the rent. He's invested in us. We matter to him.

Go back to that exercise in chapter 1 where you were invited to finish the sentence beginning, "I am. . . ." If it is true that we are not only made by God but out of God, then God has invested godly qualities in us. Whatever describes God is who we truly are. Jesus comes to protect that investment.

Deep inside of every human heart is a desire to be loved. We want to know we matter and that someone genuinely cares about us.

In the movie *Trading Places*—now over thirty years old!—Dan Akroyd plays a snobbish investor who gets scammed by his bosses. They make a bet that their protégé couldn't really survive if they took away everything he had. (Sort of a modern-day story of Job, wouldn't you agree?) They cancel his credit cards, take his identity, remove his seat in the exclusive club, and even pay his butler not to recognize him. His only hope is a prostitute played by Jamie Lee Curtis. The two meet in jail. She believes he is who he says he is, but he needs her to invest in him. She gives him her life's savings, believing he can spin it into gold in the stock market.

In one scene Curtis nurses Akroyd back to health while he is sick. He asks why she is doing this, and she replies, "I'm protecting my investment." Comparing Jesus to a movie prostitute may not be the best image, but Jesus comes to protect God's investment in us. He comes to restore who we really are. He believes in our true identity.

God says, "I gave you a sense of humor; you can make people smile. I have put something in your life that shines. I believe in you.

"I gave you the ability to inspire people. You have a way of bringing out the best in others. You are awesome. I believe in you.

"I gave you sensitivity to others. I gave you compassion. You help people keep going. I believe in you.

"I gave you wit and intellect. I gave you the ability to lead others. People depend on you. I believe in you."

The one best able to render a verdict on the qualities of your life and mine is the one who gave us those qualities. It has been said that psychologists tell us we all tend to see ourselves the way we think the most important person in our lives sees us. Now pause there before you read on. Say it again to yourself: We tend to see ourselves the way we think the most important person in our lives sees us. If a parent is the most important person in your life, you will tend to see yourself the way you think that parent sees you. If it is a spouse, a coach, a teacher, a boss, it's the same.

Therefore, why not make Jesus Christ the most important person in life? Jesus is fully invested in us. We matter to him. Jesus shows us that God has "skin in the game." He comes through the gate.

Jesus as the Door

According to some Bible translations, Jesus calls himself the *door* for the sheep. What can that different word tell us about Jesus? Sheep pens were not the only enclosure shepherds used. When they were out in the country they didn't have permanent structures built along buildings with high walls and locking gates. In the country they used sheepfolds.

Here the threats were not thieves and bandits but predatory animals like jackals, wildcats, and foxes. Shepherds used folds to keep the sheep at night. These enclosures provided walls, but the door was just a bare entrance. No gate. It was an opening in the wall for sheep to go in and out freely.

How could sheep stay protected without a door? The shepherd would lie down at night in the doorway. The shepherd would be the door. This is what people would have pictured when Jesus said, "I am the door for the sheep." I recently saw these kinds of sheep pens in the Holy Land.

Sheep are restless creatures. They are easily startled, and once startled it is hard for them to settle down and sleep. Author W. Phillip Keller spent some time as a sheep rancher in Africa and wrote a couple of books relating his experience as a shepherd to his faith in Christ, the Good Shepherd. He said four conditions have to be met in order for sheep to lie down: They must be free of fear, free from friction with others in the flock, free from parasites and pests, and free from hunger.[1]

Can you relate to being a sheep? Have you ever had anything bother you to the point you couldn't rest? Maybe a very real threat you were facing, friction with someone, or an issue that kept annoying you? You would lie down but your mind would race. So much for counting sheep.

What helps sheep to lie down? They see the shepherd in the doorway. They know that between them and the object of their worries sits the shepherd. They focus on the shepherd.

GOD'S CARE IN THE MIDST OF CRISIS

Ira Sankey was the song leader for the great evangelist D. L. Moody back in the 1800s. Christmas Eve 1875 Sankey was on a Delaware River steamboat, and other passengers recognized him. They asked him to sing a hymn, so he chose William B. Bradbury's "Savior, Like a Shepherd Lead Us." One of the stanzas began, "We are thine; do Thou befriend us. Be the Guardian of our way."

When he finished, a man asked Sankey if he had ever served in the Union Army. Mr. Sankey said he had. The man asked if he had served in a particular area in 1862. Again, Sankey said he had served there as a sentry many nights.

The man replied, "So did I, but I was serving in the Confederate army. One night I snuck up on you, raised my musket, and took aim. At that instant, just as a moment ago, you raised your eyes to heaven and began to sing. You sang the same words you did just now. I heard the words perfectly: 'We are Thine; do Thou befriend us. Be the Guardian of our way.' Those words stirred up many memories. I began to think of my childhood and my God-fearing mother. She had many times sung that song to me. When you finished it was impossible for me to take aim again. I thought, *'The Lord who is able to save that man from certain death must surely be great and mighty.'* And my arm dropped limp at my side and the gun went down."[2]

Ira Sankey had no idea how the shepherd of his soul was looking out for him one night in 1862. He had no idea of the predator that was out there. All he knew was to focus on his Good Shepherd.

We love stories like that, don't we? We love stories where God intervenes and spares somebody from trouble or pain or difficulty. We think, *That's what I want God to do for me!* But do you know what the real power of this image is? It's that even when we are surrounded by threats and not spared from pain, we can still have peace! The shepherd can still calm us in the midst of crisis.

It's hard to talk about the Good Shepherd and not think of the Twenty-third Psalm. In the fourth verse it says, "Though I walk through the valley of the shadow of death." Though I walk *through*. Leonard Sweet notes the two significant words in that sentence, *though* and *through*, and observes the one simple difference between them. The letter R.

Then Sweet points out the American Sign Language symbol for *R*—crossed fingers. In the early days of the Christian faith people made a similar gesture with their fingers. They crossed the index and middle fingers as a sign of the cross. It was a way of identifying themselves to each other. [3]

Somehow over the years crossed fingers changed meaning a bit. Many people cross fingers for good luck. They cross fingers in hopes of passing an exam, winning the lottery, or celebrating the Cubs winning a World Series. You see lots of crossed fingers in Chicago.

How did it come to mean good luck? I have a theory I can't prove, but here goes. Early Christians would cross fingers not only to identify themselves to each other but also when they were going through trials. When they didn't know how a crisis would turn out, they crossed fingers as a way of claiming Christ's presence with them, knowing he was by their side. Observers saw the people crossing their fingers walking through trials with amazing peace. I think of Stephen being stoned in Acts 8. Observers said his face looked like that of an angel. Christ turns a *though* into *through*.

Though I am facing this layoff; though I have received this bad news about my health; though my child is hurting. . . . Christ is with me. I will get through.

Perhaps over the years people connected folks who walked through trials with confidence with the fact that they crossed fingers. Like I said, I can't prove that theory but it seems plausible. Focusing on Christ makes a real difference when we go through trials because we understand him as a Good Shepherd who has our best interest at heart, who is always looking after us, and who stands between us and our worries. All we need to do is focus on him.

In the first chapter I told about a woman in a hospice center who always said, "I am so blessed." Not long after my visit that day, she passed away. At the funeral her daughter described being at the doctor's office when her mother first learned she had cancer nine years prior.

Her mother had been enjoying a revived spiritual journey, engaging in Bible studies and growth opportunities. She was an amazing witness to other people, especially young mothers. On the way home from the doctor, the daughter said to her mother, "I just don't understand why this would happen to you, why God would let it happen to you." Her mother responded, "Why not me? If God can be glorified through this, then why not?" She had found someone to focus on who gave her confidence and peace.

During the last ten days of her life, the mother wasn't able to respond. She wasn't conscious. It was like she was in a very deep sleep. People in the church had given her clutching crosses, small wooden crosses formed like the palm of your hand. While she was not aware of people around her, in both hands she held these crosses. When she died, the nurse had to pry her fingers open to remove the crosses. Her grip had been so tight that the very grain of wood was imprinted on her palms.

It reminded me of a verse from Isaiah, "I have inscribed you on the palms of my hands" (49:16). When we know how tightly God holds us, it gives us something to hold when we need it most.

Do you have something to hold onto in your life that reassures you of your true worth and value? Do you have something to hold onto that reminds you that, though trials come, you'll get through? Do you know God's faithful care?

Just keep your fingers crossed.

Reflection/Discussion Questions

Why do you think the Bible uses the image of a shepherd to describe the relationship between God and God's people?

How much are you a creature of habit? What are some of your routine habits? What are ways you seek refreshment and energy?

What does it mean to you to say, "God watches over my coming in and going out"?

What do you think is the importance of Jesus saying, "I am the Good Shepherd," versus just saying, "I am the Shepherd"?

Thinking of the "gate" as a reference to a shepherd having to rent space for protection of a flock, how is Jesus "invested" in you?

In what practical ways does it impact your life to make Jesus the most influential person in life?

Thinking too of the "door" image, have you ever felt Jesus coming between you and some potential threat?

What does it mean to focus on Christ when you are restless?

How have you experienced Christ as a Good Shepherd?

NOTES

_____

_____

_____

_____

_____

_____

_____

_____

_____

_____

_____

_____

_____

_____

_____

_____

_____

_____

_____

5

"I Am the True Vine"
Knowing God's Power

John 15:1-8

A year after Susan and I married, we moved to Matthews, North Carolina, where I had been appointed as associate pastor of a large, fast-growing church. This was our first move as a couple, made more exciting by the fact that there was no parsonage. We were going to buy our first house.

We found one in a fairly new neighborhood not far from the church. The realtor explained it was a great "starter" home. I hoped that meant it came with instructions. It did not.

One day in early November the temperature dropped and stayed below freezing—very unusual for North Carolina that time of year. Susan called me at the office saying the house was cold, and she couldn't get the furnace to work. I said, "It's simple. . . ." (Note to all new couples: When your spouse has been working on something for hours and can't figure it out, it's not wise to begin a sentence with the words, "It's simple.")

I explained, "All you need to do is turn the thermostat to 'heat.'" Silence.

After a few moments she replied in a very composed voice, "I've tried that . . . (I could hear her thoughts, *you idiot!*). Do you have any other ideas?"

I said, "The furnace isn't that old. It can't be broken. See if there is a switch on it."

Again, a few moments of composed quiet, and then she said, "I've already done that too. I can't find one."

I said, "What do you mean you can't find one? Every furnace has an on/off switch or reset button or something. You just haven't found it yet." Longer silence than before.

"Perhaps you just need to come home and see if you can figure it out since I can't."

I let out an annoyed huff. Ever done that with your spouse? You huff loud enough to communicate that you are annoyed but not so loud that you can't deny it.

Thirty minutes later I pulled in the driveway. I walked in and found Susan sitting at the kitchen table wearing every item of winter apparel she owned. I strode toward the furnace room like Captain America. I would fix this problem in a flash and get back to saving the rest of the world, hoping in the meantime to prove that it was such an obvious fix I should have never been called away in the first place. After all, it interrupted my doughnut break at the office.

Since this house had no basement, the furnace was located in a utility closet off of the kitchen. I looked for an on/off switch. No luck. Again I could hear Susan's thoughts from behind me: *See, I told you so.*

I got a flashlight and looked behind the furnace. Again, no luck. I figured these new furnaces were probably built without switches. It must be the main circuit. Fortunately we had tripped a breaker the previous week. I say it was fortunate, because I had already spent an hour that night locating the circuit panel. I found the furnace switch. It was already on. Captain America was thoroughly stumped.

Susan suggested we call a furnace repair company. She might as well have put a knife in my back. Calling the furnace people would be an admission that I was incapable, that I didn't know how to fix this problem, that I couldn't figure it out with just a little time. Forty-five minutes later I called the furnace people.

The repairman arrived and started inspecting the furnace. He looked on the wall and noticed what looked like a light switch. He flipped it up, and the furnace came on. He said, "I guess that will take care of it," and started filling out the paperwork.

I was embarrassed and frustrated. I said, "Whoever heard of a furnace having an unmarked switch on the wall like that?" He smiled and said, "You have now," and handed me a bill for $50.

All the power needed to keep a 2,000-square-foot home warm on a freezing day was an arm's reach away, and we sat cold. Ever had an experience like that? Ever been really close to a source of power but felt cut off from it? Could that ever describe you?

Sometimes in the spiritual life we can be surrounded by symbols and activities that make God's power seem as easy as flipping a switch, and yet we remain powerless. We don't need another worship service or prayer meeting or book to read (except this one, of course). Our problem is not that we are irreligious. It's that we are plenty religious and still feel disconnected from God.

For every person who has felt this way, Jesus said, "I am the vine, you are the branches. . . . Abide in me." It is a prescription for staying connected to God's power.

ENCOURAGING DISCOURAGED FOLLOWERS

As we have learned with the other "I Am" sayings, to best understand this image we need to know the context. First, consider the location of this story in the Gospel of John. It appears in what is known as the "Farewell Discourses." In this series of teachings found in John 14–17 Jesus prepares the disciples for his departure. Jesus knows he will soon be crucified. He wants to get his followers ready for what his death will mean. They will be cut off from him. Jesus knows it will be a critical time for their faith.

At one point in his ministry Jesus had told the disciples they would do greater things than he had done. Imagine hearing those words. You have witnessed Jesus feed thousands, heal the sick, and even raise the dead. He says you will do even greater things! But when he is suddenly gone, how tempting would it be to give up? It would be easy to say, "I don't have that kind of power. I can't do those things. I might as well quit."

Jesus offers an image to help those who feel they have a lot to live up to and get frustrated by their own frailty.

THE SIGNIFICANCE OF A VINE

Again, as with the other "I Am" sayings, the history of Israel provides an important context. When Jesus said, "I am the Bread of Life," it was in response to a discussion about the manna in the wilderness. When he said, "I am the Light of the World," he was attending the Feast of Tabernacles. Even the Good Shepherd saying evokes images of the priests and kings of Israel who were called to shepherd God's people.

Now Jesus says, "I am the True Vine." The grapevine was an oft-used symbol of Israel. Lots of Old Testament passages speak of Israel being God's vineyard. "The vineyard of the LORD of hosts is the house of Israel, and the people of Judah are his pleasant planting" (Isa. 5:7). "I planted you as a choice vine, . . . from the purest stock. How then did you turn degenerate and become a wild vine?" (Jer. 2:21). "You brought a vine out of Egypt; you drove out the nations and planted it" (Ps. 80:8).

The grapevine came to symbolize the nation of Israel much like an eagle symbolizes America. Even the entrance to the Temple provided a visual reminder: Over the doorway a giant grapevine with grape clusters was carved and covered in pure gold. It is said that the grapes were the size of a person's head! A replica of the entrance to the Temple verifies this.

The grapevine came to symbolize the nation of Israel much like an eagle symbolizes America.

Jesus could well have been standing under this carving shortly before uttering this "I Am" saying. The implication is clear: Jesus is connected to Israel's source of strength.

Do you know that many modern-day grapevines have an ancestry? Some wine-producing grapevines in France can be traced back to the twelfth century. Many vineyards in California started with vines brought from Europe. Viticulturists understand that the quality of fruit passes down through the vine.

When Jesus says, "I am the True Vine" he is indicating that the same authority and power of God given to Israel lives in him; but then he declares, "I Am." He is not just a son of Israel; he is the Son of God, connected to the true, or real, source of Israel's strength.

We stay connected to God's power by staying connected to Christ. The way to do this is to *abide*. That word appears ten times in John 15. Abiding in Christ is the key to experiencing spiritual power. How do we abide in Christ? Jesus offers a vivid image—be a branch!

For the remainder of this chapter I want you to imagine being a branch. Not the vine or the fruit—but the branch. If you are reading this alone just stretch out your arms like a branch. On one side feel yourself connected to the vine. Imagine grabbing hold of the vine. On the other side, imagine that you are holding up fruit. You're a branch! Yes, you look silly, but you are a branch.

What does being a branch have to do with staying spiritually healthy?

THE POWER OF PRUNING

For one thing, branches get pruned. Ouch!

Jesus said, "God is like a vinegrower." Sometimes the vinegrower prunes the vines. Pruning means removing excessive growth that robs the vine of its energy.

I love growing vegetables. While serving my first church, I identified a place in the backyard of the parsonage where I could plant a vegetable garden. I borrowed a tiller from a church member and dug up the ground. In the spring I planted lettuce, squash, zucchini, potatoes, and tomatoes . . . especially tomatoes. I lived in a big tomato-growing region. Some of the commercial farmers in the area grew tomatoes that were shipped around the world. People there knew how to grow tomatoes.

We stay connected to God's power by staying connected to Christ.

When my plants started producing fruit I decided to show off my gardening skills to a retired church member whom I knew to be an excellent gardener. He scanned my patch and lingered over the tomato plants. After a moment he looked up and said, "Preacher, don't forget to pinch the suckers."

"Pinch the what?" I asked.

The man repeated the phrase and showed me what he was talking about. He pointed out the growth stalks shooting out between the branches and vine. He said those were suckers and not to be confused with the limbs that produce fruit.

He told me, "If you don't pinch off these shoots, they will sap energy from the vine. It will lessen the quality of the fruit. Pinch your suckers, preacher."

Now think about this in a spiritual light. Do you have any suckers in your life? Are there activities or relationships that sap your energy but don't really promise to be productive? Do you ever feel that the real priorities in your life do not get the time and attention they need?

"I am the vine, you are the branches. Those who abide in me and I in them bear much fruit, because apart from me you can do nothing."

JOHN 15:5

If so, you might want to try this exercise, a "pinching the suckers" practice. You could call it a Spiritual Energy Audit. Write down the areas of your life that deserve your greatest energy. What are they? Certainly there is self and self-care. That probably takes the most time. Think about how much time you need to spend asleep to keep your body rested, time for recreation to keep yourself refreshed, and time for spiritual devotion and prayer to keep your relationship with God strong. These are all activities that you need to do to maintain and nurture yourself.

What about other areas deserving prime energy—family, friends, work? Are there specific aspects of your work that should be higher priorities than others? Perhaps activities where you want to give your best? List them and estimate the hours or percentage of your week you give to those activities in a devoted way. These are the important fruits.

Now list everything else—the activities that rob you of your best energy: tasks you know you need to delegate, work not directly related to your gifts and primary purpose, time spent waiting, watching television, unnecessary meetings, emailing and surfing the Internet, and so forth.

How do they line up? Do your time and energy get apportioned appropriately?

True confession: Every time I take this audit I discover parts of my life that are out of balance. I find suckers that need to be pinched. It's not always about the amount of time I spend but what happens to my energy in those times. An hour listening to someone fuss and fume about a church issue can suck away the remainder of my energy for the day. An argument with a family member (usually because of too little time together) can sap my productivity at work.

Recently I did this audit one morning at my desk and realized I was not spending enough time with my high-school-aged daughters. My middle daughter, Sarah, was deciding which college to attend. I texted her, "Let's get coffee after school today."

She texted back, "Ummm, OK."

I met her at home, and we went to a new coffee shop I had discovered. We got seated with our drinks and she said, "Dad, why are we here?"

I said, "I just want to see how you're doing, find out how it's going with your decision making, and see if I can help." We talked for a little bit, and then an awkward silence descended.

Finally Sarah said, "Dad, this is weird."

Sarah's comment was an indictment of my failure to spend more time with my daughter. When you spend time with someone frequently, it isn't freaky. I just have to remember to pinch the suckers every now and then. As I said, it's not just about assessing where our time goes. It is about realizing what happens to us in that time. Let's say you have to do a certain activity, but you resent it. You find when you do this activity it leaves you drained and in a poor mood. It means you have to be careful about what you schedule after such activities.

Doing this kind of time audit may lead to changing your schedule or changing how you approach certain things. When our kids were a little younger my wife spent a lot of time in in the car, driving the kids around. She called it the "mommy taxi." The task usually left her frustrated because it was not productive time, especially when she was by herself either on the way to pick up a child or following a drop-off.

Then my wife started using that time for calling friends or people she wanted to "visit" while in the car. She'd schedule phone meetings during that time. She'd even use it to play praise music and pray (with eyes open, of course!).

The key is this: No one else will do the pruning for us. Wayne Cordeiro, founding pastor of New Hope Christian Fellowship in Honolulu, calls pruning "protecting our five percent."[1] Nearly 95 percent of what we do in life others can do. One day someone else will do our job, take care of our house, volunteer in our place, and so forth. No one else, however, can be a husband or wife to our spouse, a father or mother to our child(ren), take care of our bodies, or tend our souls. It's up to us to do the necessary and regular pruning of our schedules.

When we prune something, we are not saying it is unimportant. We are just keeping productive things productive.

The Value of Cutting Away

At other times the gardener cuts away dead branches completely. These are the branches that aren't growing. They are dead. They don't have the hope of producing. They just weigh down the vine.

Again, let's make a spiritual application. What nonproductive branches might we identify in our personal lives?

- Regrets?
- Living in the past?
- Resentments?
- Bitterness?
- Envy?

Dead limbs can't sap energy from the vine, but it takes energy to keep them propped up. Holding on to heavy weight takes a lot of effort; the limbs must be cut away.

Some counselors say depression works this way. When we are depressed, it sometimes means we are suppressing feelings. We are holding something inside, afraid or unwilling to let it out. We don't want to admit we are resentful or angry, so we stuff it down. It takes energy to suppress and hold in these emotions, energy that robs us of feeling alive.

In his book *Messy Spirituality,* Mike Yaconelli tells the story of Margaret, a woman who lived nearly forty years trying to overcome the pain of what happened to her one day as a little girl. She attended a one-room schoolhouse and from her first day she collided with the demanding and difficult teacher, Ms. Garner. Their relationship continued to spiral downward until completely crashing one particular day.

Ms. Garner, pushed beyond her limit by Margaret's lateness to class one more time, decided to teach Margaret a lesson in the most cruel way. She instructed the students to come up to the chalkboard one by one and write something bad about Margaret. The students filed forward and wrote their statements: "Margaret is stupid!" "Margaret is selfish." "Margaret is a dummy." "Margaret is fat."

The pain of that day did not leave her. Forty years later Margaret was still trying to rid herself of the wounds she suffered that day. She spent two years in weekly therapy, trying to cut away the memories that caused decades of anxiety and depression. In her last counseling session, the counselor led Margaret to remember each of the twenty-five children and what they wrote about her. Through many tears and much pain, she recounted each name and each statement. When she had finished crying, her counselor informed her that she had forgotten one person. Margaret protested. She knew she had not forgotten anyone, so many times had she remembered and recounted that day. The counselor insisted.

> "No, Margaret. You did forget someone. See, he's sitting in the back of the classroom. He's standing up, walking toward your teacher, Ms. Garner. She is handing him a piece of chalk and he's taking it, Margaret, he's taking it! Now he's walking over to the blackboard and picking up an eraser. *He is erasing every one of the sentences the students wrote.* They are gone! Margaret, they are gone! Now he's turning and looking at you, Margaret. Do you recognize him yet? Yes, his name is Jesus. Look, he's writing new sentences on the board.

'Margaret is loved. Margaret is beautiful. Margaret is gentle and kind. Margaret is strong. Margaret has great courage.'

And Margaret began to weep. But very quickly, the weeping turned into a smile, and then into laughter, and then into tears of joy."[2]

It is a dramatic story to be sure. We may not have experiences of this kind that need to be cut away, but if God's power can be found in this kind of pain, then certainly it can be found in lesser challenges. There's hope for everyone.

CLINGING TO THE VINE

Two ways of staying connected to Christ involve (1) removing what is unnecessary in our lives, and (2) staying focused on the vine. Again, imagine being a branch. Are your arms getting tired?

On one side we have the vine, our life source. On the other side we have fruit. Our effectiveness is determined by which one we focus on, and in our world it's hard not to focus on the fruit. So much of our worth is measured by what we produce. We can feel pretty good when we are producing well, but when we aren't . . . well, that's another story.

We also measure ourselves by comparing our fruit to what others produce. We can feel fine until we look around. Focusing on the success, achievements, and appearance of others can undo us.

Our job is to be a branch and let God's power flow through us.

We can obsess over fruit. We start to believe that the fruit is up to us. But Jesus says it's not. That's not our job. Our job is to be a branch and let God's power flow through us. Sounds simple, but it can get confusing, especially when we start to draw our self-worth from our fruit. Our fruit and how it compares with others begins to determine our identity. We begin to think we are the vine and are our own source of strength. We have to ask ourselves, "Do I receive my identity from the things I produce or the One who produces through me?"

When I was thirty-two, I got confused about this. I went to my first senior pastor appointment at Lake Junaluska, North Carolina, the location of one of the finest United Methodist retreat centers. World leaders in the church frequently attended our church services. Not only that, many retired ministers and bishops lived nearby. I started worrying about the quality of my preaching and how good I wanted it to be.

The parsonage where our family lived stood right beside the church. On Saturday nights my routine was to go to the office and put finishing touches on the sermon, print it out, and then go to the sanctuary alone to pray. My prayers usually went something like this . . . "Dear God, *pleeasse* bless this sermon. Please make it great." *Please* was a word I used a lot in those prayers. But one Saturday night my prayer was interrupted. I felt God whisper words in my spirit that changed my life.

God said: "What is important is not the quality of the material you give me to use but my power to use what you give me."

That simple statement transformed me. It didn't mean work less. It meant fret less. It meant that my work is simply to let God work through me.

I have to be reminded of that regularly, because I frequently lose sight of the fact that my job is to be a branch. When I get overwhelmed by challenges or needs in the church and start to fret over the answers I'm looking for or tasks to do, I must cling to the vine.

What is important is not the quality of the material you give me to use but my power to use what you give me.

It's been almost twenty years since that experience. One recent Sunday, following the final service of the morning, a woman came up to me. The sermon that day had explored following our life's purpose and being open for God to use us. The woman was distraught. She had been trying to do just that but was frustrated because God had not shown her what she was supposed to be doing with her life.

I said, "Okay, let's simplify. Let's make our purpose in life to honor God and stop there. Wherever you are, just say, 'I make it my purpose to honor God right where I am now.' If you make that your purpose, then wherever you are is a place you can honor God. Right now you are in the place where you can fulfill your purpose. And if you honor God, then you are in the right place. Just make honoring God your aim."

As the woman thanked me and walked away, I kind of patted myself on the back for helping this person. I turned to walk out of a now empty sanctuary and felt God whisper, "And do you believe you do that, Rob? Will you do that? Will you focus solely on honoring me right where you are?" I had been wrestling with challenges in the church, fretting over problems without clear answers. I was invited to clutch the vine all over again.

Do you still have your arms up? (You didn't expect to get a workout while reading this book, did you?) Again picture the vine on one side. On the other is the fruit. Which way do you look most of the time? Is it toward the goals you are trying to accomplish? The tasks you have to do? The activities that keep your life fuller than you want? The demands you would like to get beyond but can't seem to get rid of? Or do you look toward the vine?

When we focus on the vine, we raise a white flag of surrender. We admit we can't produce everything we ideally would like. We admit we need help. Sometimes help comes in the form of God's pruning. Sometimes God cuts away whatever we don't need. All the time, we need to remember that God is responsible for producing the fruit. Our job is to be a branch.

Okay, you can put your arms down now.

Reflection/Discussion Questions

When was a time you felt near to God but far away from God's presence? (Perhaps you were going to church regularly or carrying out lots of religious functions, but you didn't feel power in your faith.)

What do you think is the meaning of a grapevine as a symbol for the nation of Israel?

What did Jesus mean by saying, "I am the True Vine"?

If pruning helps a branch stay healthy, what does it mean for us to be pruned? When was a time you felt pruned?

Are less important things robbing you of productive energy? If so, what are they?

Can you relate to holding on to dead things that don't have the chance to produce? Resentment? A disappointment? Shame?

What does it mean to you to "cling to the vine"? Have you ever placed more focus on being fruitful than being faithful?

Notes

_____

_____

_____

_____

_____

_____

_____

_____

_____

_____

_____

_____

_____

_____

_____

_____

_____

_____

6

"I Am the Way, the Truth, and the Life"
Knowing God's Way

John 14:1-7

This is the "I Am" saying that troubles me most. Jesus said, "I am the Way, and the Truth, and the Life." If the Gospel stopped at those words, that would be one thing, but it continues: "No one comes to the Father except through me." That's where the trouble begins. That single verse has been a major source of controversy for centuries, perhaps since this Gospel was first accepted as scripture. It is used by some Christians to invalidate other religions. Sometimes it is employed as a weapon, justifying mistreatment and even abuse toward people of other faiths.

Instead of driving people into the church, this text has driven many away. The narrowness and intolerance implied by these verses cause open-minded, accepting individuals to reject the claims of the Christian faith, or at least the church.

Consider the way some have interpreted a story from the early life of Karl Marx. Marx grew up in a Jewish family in Prussia. His father converted to Christianity before Marx was born, even changing his first name from the Jewish Herschel to a more German sounding Heinrich. He did this so his business would prosper in the predominantly Christian village where the family lived.

Some modern Christians have interpreted that act as shameless exploitation of religion for personal gain. Because Karl Marx saw the shame and pretense of it, so they say, he later concluded that all religion is an opiate.

History actually records the story differently. Yes, his father converted but not for gain. It was for survival. You see, Christians in this little village felt this Jewish businessman must convert. After all, the Bible is clear. There is no way to God except through Christ. So villagers silently boycotted his business and shunned his family as a way of influencing him toward the Christian faith. He converted in order for his family to live.

Which version of the story do you think had greater power to turn someone away from religion?

At the other extreme, some Christians avoid John 14:6 altogether. They feel it is imperative to show respect to all people regardless of their beliefs. After all, as many loving people reason, isn't it right for Christians to be kind and respectful?

Yet, as the old saying goes, "Ignoring what someone said doesn't mean they didn't say it!" Jesus makes a significant claim about himself in these verses. In many ways John's Gospel is built around this claim. To ignore it seems irresponsible if we are to take the Bible seriously.

How are we to make sense of John 14:6? To begin with, let's consider what these words might have meant to Jesus' hearers and think about what John wanted those first readers of his Gospel to know. Then, in light of that, let's think about what this claim says to us today. In other words: What did it mean then? And what does it mean now?

INTERPRETING JOHN 14:6

Jesus was not speaking to a large, diverse audience. He was talking to his disciples. In the sequence of events in John's Gospel, the words were spoken in the upper room following the last supper. There were not people of other faiths or religions in the crowd. There were no Greeks, Romans, Buddhists, or Hindus. He was talking to his closest followers.

Jesus said to him, "I am the way, and the truth, and the life. No one comes to the Father except through me."

JOHN 14:6

Jesus had just delivered very hard news. He was about to depart from this world. The passage begins with the familiar words, "Do not let your hearts be troubled. Believe in God, believe also in me. In my Father's house there are many dwelling places." We often hear these words at funerals because they comfort mourners. Comfort was the intent when Jesus spoke them to the disciples. Jesus presents a picture of heaven. But notice how Jesus describes it. "In my Father's house there are many dwelling places." Some translations say *rooms* or even *mansions*. The word is the noun form of the verb *abide*. We talked about that in the last chapter. Ten times in John 15 Jesus told his followers to "abide in me" like a branch abides in the vine. Jesus' picture of heaven is a place of perfect abiding with him—no more separation from God.

Then Jesus says to his followers, "You know the way to the place where I am going." The disciple Thomas, known for his doubting, probably should be remembered for his courage to ask questions. He speaks up, "Lord, we're not sure where you are going; how can we know the way?" Jesus says, "I am the way."

In other words, Jesus isn't arguing which religion is the right one. For goodness sake, you can make the point that Jesus wasn't even trying to start a religion! He isn't making a case for himself over other faiths. He is reassuring his followers that in him they have connection to heaven. He is their access to God.

UNDERSTANDING THE SETTING OF JOHN'S GOSPEL

Commentators also point out what was going on when John wrote this Gospel. It was the last of the Gospels to be written, probably at the end of the first century. By this time tensions between Jews and Christians were on the verge of erupting. Nearly forty years after Jesus' death, Israel revolted against Rome and was defeated. Many Christians didn't join in the revolt. Jews started to question the national loyalty and patriotism of Christians. In many places Christians were turned away from the synagogue. They were cut off from the one place that made them feel connected to God and God's people.

Add to that the fact that Christians also became targets of persecution by Romans. Ever since Emperor Nero set Rome on fire in 64 CE and blamed it on Christians, the last half of the first century saw increased persecution toward Christians throughout the empire. This culminated with Emperor Domitian's violent treatment of Christians at the turn of the century. Scholars believe that the book of Revelation was written in order to encourage believers persecuted under Domitian. Christians were betwixt and between. They were no longer accepted by their fellow citizens and considered enemies of the state by Rome.

In her commentary on John, New Testament scholar Gail R. O'Day says, "It is incumbent upon the contemporary interpreter to engage in an act of theological imagination."[1] This imagination involves trying to understand the world in which the Gospel was written and how that might influence our understanding of Jesus' words. In a world where their belief was in the minority, early Christians needed confirmation that their faith was valid. John 14:6 affirms their faith.

That fuller context helps us understand not only how Jesus might have intended these words for his hearers at the time but also why they would have been included in a Gospel written three-quarters of a century after he said them. Instead of being used as weapons to convince others they are wrong, these words were meant to assure Christ-followers that their faith was genuine, their connection to Christ real, and their path one that leads to the Father.

But, and this is a big but, that still doesn't minimize the exclusive nature of these words: "No one comes to the Father except through me." How are we to understand them?

It is reported that C. S. Lewis once arrived late to a gathering of religious scholars in London and found everyone in lively debate. He asked the cause of all the hubbub. Someone explained that they were discussing the distinctiveness of Christianity among other religions. Without much hesitation Lewis said, "Oh, that's easy."

The room quieted down as people listened. After all it was a rather presumptuous thing to say in such an esteemed crowd of brilliant colleagues who were having no easy time answering the question. "So enlighten us, Mr. Lewis," someone invited. "What makes Christianity distinct?" Lewis answered, "It's grace."[2]

Concepts of forgiveness are not missing in other religions, nor is compassion absent. The point of Lewis's statement is that God's grace is wholly responsible for drawing us to God, not our actions. What ultimately merits getting into heaven is not our work but God's grace. That is what I think Jesus means when he says, "No one comes to the Father except through me." Our salvation, our getting into heaven does not depend on what we do. It is not merit-based. Salvation comes through grace. It is as exclusive as that; and yet, it is as inclusive as that. God can appropriate God's grace to whomever God wants.

Think about it for a moment. The way many Christians use this verse negates the need for grace. The statement is interpreted as a required belief: Jesus is the way. So, the reasoning goes that our knowing, accepting, and believing is what gets us into heaven. What is the common denominator there? What *we* know, accept, and believe.

I am not saying that knowing, accepting, and believing are unnecessary; our understanding and acceptance of what God has done through Jesus Christ is essential. Yet, the emphasis of John 14:6 seems to be focused on our understanding and deciding whether or not we believe Jesus is the *only* way. But Jesus doesn't use the word *only*, and he does use the word *way*. What seems to be more important to Jesus than *believing* is *being*. Living in his way is what matters.

God can appropriate God's grace to whomever God wants.

Yet, my previous question still stands: How are we to understand Jesus' saying "no one comes to the Father except through me"? That still sounds pretty exclusive. Let me answer a question with a question. What if the way of Christ is bigger than the name of Christ? What if the truth of Jesus is bigger than the words we use? *(Okay, that was two questions.)*

Sometimes when I am talking to groups about this passage, I reorganize the letters in the name *Jesus* and ask, "What if his name had been, 'Sejus?' or 'Sujes?' or 'Jusse?' Would that have changed who Jesus was or is? Of course not. It is the person who gives meaning to the name, not the other way around.

Obviously, when we emphasize the name of Jesus, it is not the name but the person who is important. In other languages, that name is different anyway. The proper name in Hebrew is *Yeshua*, which means "God is salvation." Jesus is Jesus because he is the embodiment of a grand truth—God is salvation. Jesus came to live out that truth and provide a way for us to experience it.

That way is a way of grace and truth. It is not limited to our ability to explain or even understand it. It is larger than our spelling! What if

God's path of salvation is as narrow as the person of Jesus Christ, but as wide as God's mercy?

In his book *Love Wins*, Rob Bell writes about John 14:6:

> This is as wide and expansive a claim as a person can make. What [Jesus] doesn't say is how, or when, or in what manner the mechanism functions that gets people to God through him. He doesn't even state that those coming to the Father through him will even know that they are coming exclusively through him. He simply claims that whatever God is doing in the world to know and redeem and love and restore the world is happening through him. . . . He is as exclusive as himself and as inclusive as containing every single particle in creation.[3]

Our salvation is up to God. Accepting Christ does not mean we have to become narrow, intolerant people. In fact, it should make us just the opposite.

WHAT DOES JOHN 14:6 MEAN FOR US?

And that brings us to the next question, what do these words from the Gospel of John mean for us today? When we stop looking at them as doctrine it helps. In other words, Jesus didn't say, "No one comes to the Father except through Christianity." He didn't say, "No one comes except through the church." He said, "No one comes except through me!" We are invited to make Jesus Christ our way. He is our pattern for living.

How do we do that? We see four ways in which the first disciples made Jesus their way. First of all, they stayed connected with Jesus in a small community. That is what they did for three years. They lived with Jesus in a small group. Knowing him was not limited to individual experiences. Faith will always be somewhat abstract until it becomes real to us in relationship with other people. The disciples came to understand who Jesus was and what he could do through a fellowship with others with whom they entrusted their lives.

We are invited to make Jesus Christ our way. He is our pattern for living.

In May of 2013 Dallas Willard passed away. He was a brilliant author on the topic of Christian spirituality. In his book *The Spirit of the Disciplines*, he wrote,

> Personalities united can contain more of God and sustain the force of his greater presence much better than scattered individuals. The fire of God kindles higher as the brands are heaped together and each is warmed by the other's flame.[4]

Fellowship is no modern invention. It is as old as Jesus and twelve followers.

A second way the disciples patterned their lives after Jesus was to develop practices that deepened their connection to God. The one request the disciples made of Jesus was to teach them how to pray. They saw in his prayer life something they wanted. Living in the Jesus way means developing habits that bring us closer to God: habits such as prayer, Bible study, meditation, journaling, fasting, and other spiritual practices.

Again, Dallas Willard clarified the role and power of spiritual disciplines in our life with God: "Any activity that is in our power and enables us to achieve by grace what we cannot achieve by direct effort is a discipline of the spiritual life."[5] In other words, I might not be able to make myself more patient or understanding, but I can pray. Praying lies within my power, and over time I can see what God can do in and through me in terms of making me more patient and understanding.

Third, adopting the Jesus' way also meant practicing sacrifice. The disciples experienced the cross. They understood that new life and hope came through sacrifice. That profoundly changed them. They all made sacrifices for what they believed, yet they experienced profound joy in sacrificing.

I saw the joy in sacrifice from a woman with a beautiful spirit in my first church. She wasn't dirt poor, but she was not far from it. She heated her home exclusively with a wood stove because she couldn't afford heating fuel.

While I was serving that church, a man in the congregation volunteered to go with a conference building team to Africa. We raised funds to support him. The woman brought me a check for two hundred dollars. I told her I couldn't accept it because I knew how much she needed that money. Besides, we would be able to raise the needed funds. She persisted saying, "Please don't deny me this joy." I can't forget her words.

Some people would hear that and say, "Wait a minute. Do you mean that's the level of sacrifice you have to have in order to be a Christian?"

Not at all. At the same time, though, have you ever known people who can afford just about anything under the sun except joy? They would give about anything if they could have joy, but somehow it eludes them.

The disciples of Jesus knew there are some things in this world money can't buy. They found living a life of sacrifice bought something priceless.

Fourth, the disciples showed compassion to people . . . all people. Making Jesus their way meant they had to release their prejudices. They reached out to people they would otherwise have avoided.

This also meant noticing folks they were able to help. Following Jesus made them aware of how he noticed people that others over-looked. When you make Jesus your way, this is what happens. You become open to Jesus pointing out opportunities to extend grace to others.

My wife, Susan, on her way home one Monday stopped by Wal-Mart to pick up a few things. As she stood in the checkout line she had an experience of God's presence. "I sensed God was in that little space with me, and I felt God telling me, 'Pay attention to the person in front of you. Just observe him.'" So Susan just started watching the man.

He was a young father with two little children. The kids were rambunctious—the father was trying to tend to them and put his purchases on the counter. Susan noticed he was buying a microwave oven and a couple of really big laundry baskets. She wondered what that meant. *Could it be*, she thought, *he doesn't have a way to cook meals? That he needs a simple way to heat up food to give his children at home? Or does it mean he doesn't have much time to cook and needs a quick way to feed them?*

As she looked at the laundry baskets she saw that they were really big ones and wondered, *Does he have to go to a laundromat, so he needs containers large enough to carry all the clothes back and forth?*

She asked, "Can I help you? Can I hold one of your children while you check out?"

With relief he responded, "Oh, that would be great."

While Susan was holding one of the children, he put the items on the counter, checked out, and put the items in the cart. She handed his child back to him. He stepped off to the side to zip up the children's coats before going outside. Susan checked out and as she was walking past him said, "Have a good day!"

The man looked up at her while he was tying his children's shoes and said, "Ma'am, could you help me find a better job?"

She wondered, *Why would someone ask that of a total stranger? What would prompt him to do so?*

She answered, "I don't know. I don't know anybody looking for workers. I wish I could hire you. What do you do?"

The man shared some of his skills and then said, "Look, the truth is I'll do anything. I will work hard and do whatever's needed." So she got his contact information and promised to call if she learned anything.

The next day happened to be a first Tuesday of the month when our church leaders are invited to join the staff for a weekly chapel service. During the prayer concerns one of the leaders said, "I've started up a new business, and I'm looking for new employees. If you know anybody who needs a job. . . ."

Susan sat there flabbergasted. She talked to the member and gave him the contact information of the man she met in Wal-Mart. A couple of days later she received a message from our member saying, "I interviewed your person. I hired him. He's going to be making twice what he did before."

Isn't it a cool thing when you get to see God at work! But it is cooler still when you get to participate in it. That's what it means to make Jesus our way. We're not just making Jesus a way, we make him *our* way. We let it define our living and what we do, and that's how we experience God's power. This isn't just something to believe in; it's something to live out. We worship a living God who is active and moving and present and doing something right now. Think about what it means to believe that—right this minute God is seeking to do something and seeking someone through whom to do it!

God becomes real as Jesus lives in us. Most Christians don't have a hard time believing in the incarnation; we readily accept that God became flesh in Jesus. The difficulty is being God's incarnational presence for others.

STILL A GOOD QUESTION

Over one hundred years ago, Charles Sheldon wrote a book called *In His Steps*. It begins in a sleepy little church where a man down on his luck goes to worship one morning. At the end of the service he walks down front to explain to the congregation how he had sought their help but couldn't find any. He wasn't being mean, just stating his experience. Suddenly he collapsed and was taken to the hospital, where he died.

The pastor is shaken by the whole episode. He preaches about it the next Sunday. He challenges his congregation for a whole year to live with the words, "What Would Jesus Do?" This is where that expression comes from, a book written in 1897.

Today, that phrase has been bandied about quite a bit. You even see it on bracelets and jewelry. It has become almost too familiar to us, yet following Christ still comes down to that. It means being willing to live with a simple question—what would Jesus do in my shoes? What does it mean to live the Jesus way in my everyday life?

Every morning when you wake up, as soon as your feet hit the floor, say this prayer: "Jesus, what would you have me do today?"

The Reformation leader Martin Luther said, "We are to be little Christs." That is what true believing looks like, letting Christ live through us.

According to the book of Acts, the early community of Christ followers was known as "the Way" (Acts 9:2). That's a telling statement. Did it mean that people noticed that this community lived as Jesus did, following his way of life? Following the Way still means living the way of Jesus. People living like Jesus is what draws others to the Christian faith.

As you seek to follow the way of Jesus, I invite you to try a simple exercise this week. Every morning when you wake up, as soon as your feet hit the floor, say this prayer: "Jesus, what would you have me do today?"

Reflection/Discussion Questions

How have you heard people use Jesus' words "No one comes to the Father except through me"?

Remember that Jesus did not say these words to a large crowd but to his twelve disciples. Knowing the dialogue that precedes Jesus' words "I am the way, and the truth, and the life," how does that shape your understanding of this "I Am" saying?

Think too about the audience for whom the Gospel is written— perhaps Christians who have endured or are possibly facing, persecution for their faith. How do you think John wanted readers of his Gospel to understand Jesus' words here?

How do you relate to this idea of "way" as referring to right living versus right belief? How does this understanding impact your interpretation of John 14:6?

What is the difference between a church that focuses on helping people know Jesus versus a church that focuses on making people members?

What do you think it meant for the disciples to make Jesus a way of life?

How do you make Jesus a way of life in your ordinary living? What does that look like for you?

Notes

NOTES

7

"I Am the Resurrection and the Life"
Knowing God's Possibilities

John 11:17-26

Jesus didn't do Lazarus any favors. He brought Lazarus back to life, but eventually Lazarus would die again. What a bummer! It's bad enough to die one time, but to do it twice?

It gets worse. By bringing Lazarus back to life, Jesus made him an enemy of the state, as shown in the next chapter of John, "So the chief priests planned to put Lazarus to death as well, since it was on account of him that many of the Jews were deserting and were believing in Jesus" (12:10-11). Talk about tough. You get raised from the dead, and people want to kill you for it!

Yet this story is not really about Lazarus. After all, very little of it deals with Lazarus directly. Sure, he was brought back to life, but most of the narrative and attention are devoted to his sisters, Martha and Mary. In other words, the story centers on those who have to live with death. Lazarus was dead, but the sisters were the loved ones who had to face this reality.

This story is for those who have to live with death.

The longer we live the more we learn this. I was nineteen years old when the reality of death hit me in a big way for the first time. I got a call that my good friend David Cook had died. David was several years older. I had met him the first night I attended a Boy Scout meeting. He was senior patrol leader. He took me and another first-time attender and began working with us on our Tenderfoot Badge. The three of us became fast friends.

Following his graduation David became a paramedic. One day he responded to a call of a possible drowning in a river. Heavy rain in recent days had caused the river to rise; it was swollen and rushing fast. David was in a patrol boat when he saw a shoe surface. Without hesitating he dove into the murky water. He never came back up. The autopsy revealed he had a rare heart condition and went into arrest as he tried to swim against the current.

I remember the shock I felt when I got the call. There was no way David Cook could be dead. Impossible! Someone can't die at twenty-four years old, someone so good and decent.

I spent the next hour staring at a wall.

TRUSTING GOD'S PROMISE

David was a member of the Moravian church. I used to play in his church band for Easter sunrise services. To this day I can't get through an Easter weekend without remembering those high school years of playing in the sunrise services at Old Salem, North Carolina, where twenty to thirty thousand people would attend.

Some months after his funeral I pulled up beside the cemetery. I stood at his grave and just asked God, "Why? Why weren't you there, Lord? Why does such a good person who was devoting his life to helping others, leave this world so early?" I was learning to live with death.

My question wasn't that different from what Martha exclaimed to Jesus when he arrived in Bethany. "Lord, if you had been here, my brother would not have died." Have you ever said those words to God? "Lord, if you had just been here. . . ."

"If you had just been here things would be different."

. . . this accident would not have happened.

. . . this injustice would not have occurred.

. . . I would still have my job.

. . . the car wouldn't have skidded off the road.

. . . that attack would have been prevented.

There's no end to the reasons for saying, "Lord, if you had been here. . . ." This story is for those who have to live with death.

Jesus said to her, "I am the resurrection and the life. Those who believe in me, even though they die, will live, and everyone who lives and believes in me will never die."

JOHN 11:25-26

Jesus talks to Martha about her brother rising again. Martha responds, "I know that he will rise again in the resurrection on the last day."

Now where did Martha get the idea of resurrection? This may surprise you, but the idea of resurrection didn't start with Jesus. A concept of resurrection already existed in Judaism. We see it as far back as the book of Daniel. "Many of those who sleep in the dust of the earth shall awake, some to everlasting life" (12:2).

It was a belief held by the Pharisees in Jesus' day. But it was just an idea, a belief, not a reality. It was like believing something will be in the future, and between now and then we just have to gut it out. "Oh, I know he will rise again in the resurrection at the last day," says Mary. She could have added, "But that's not much good right now!"

Then Jesus drops the hammer: "*I am the resurrection and the life. Those who believe in me, even though they die, will live, and everyone who lives and believes in me shall never die.*"

Episcopal priest and author Barbara Brown Taylor says the important word in these sentences is not *resurrection* or *life* but *believe*. In Greek it is the word *pisteuo,* which also means *trust*. Typically it is translated "believe," as is normally done four times in John 11:25-26.[1]

There's a difference between believing in something and trusting in it. We truly believe someone when we are able to put our trust fully in that person.

Jesus said to her, "I am the resurrection and the life. Those who *believe* in me, even though they die, will live, and everyone who lives and *believes* in me will never die. Do you *believe* this?" She said to him, "Yes, Lord, I believe" (*emphasis added*).

Now, read it again substituting the word *trust:*

Jesus said to her, "I am the resurrection and the life. Those who *trust* in me, even though they die, will live, and everyone who lives and *trusts* in me will never die. Do you *trust* this?" She said to him, "Yes, Lord, I *trust*."

That puts a different spin on it doesn't it? There's a difference between believing in something and trusting in it. We truly believe someone when we are able to put our trust fully in that person.

Karl Barth, the famed Swiss Reformed theologian of the twentieth century, compared his relationship with God to a man who had a job ringing the bell in the center of the village. One evening he climbed the circular stairway up the bell tower. As he got near the top he lost his balance and started to fall into the dark abyss. He reached out to grab the handrail but instead his arm found the rope of the bell. He grabbed it and pulled down to steady himself. Then he heard the loud gong peal out, shattering the silence of the still night.[2]

That story became a powerful metaphor for Barth's relationship with God. It was in those times of desperation when he felt there was nowhere else to turn that he discovered the sureness of God's presence. The great goal of the spiritual life is not only to *believe* in God but to *believe* God. It is a trust issue.

EXPECTING NEW POSSIBILITIES

When I came to St. Luke's United Methodist Church in Indianapolis, I had the privilege of following Dr. Kent Millard, the highly energetic, compassionate senior pastor who had led the church for eighteen years. Kent announced his retirement the Sunday after Christmas in 2010, just a few months after learning his wife had terminal cancer. They hoped to have several years together to enjoy family and travel, but by September 2011 she passed away.

One day, several months after his wife's death, Kent had a significant experience while driving. Suddenly he felt God giving him tremendous peace. He didn't understand it. How could he be at peace? His wife had just died. He couldn't be at peace. In fact, he realized he had some resistance to being at peace, but in that moment he felt God was saying to him, "It's okay to be at peace."

Shortly after that, new possibilities started emerging. The bishop called Kent and asked him to help lead a conference initiative in stewardship. Then he was invited to go to Denver and serve three months as an interim pastor of the largest United Methodist church in that conference.

One Sunday during that time he preached about this experience. He said our own resistance can hold us back from experiencing God's possibilities, but when we accept, new opportunities can unfold. He explained how we can be resistant to new possibilities because we want to hold onto the old; but at some point there has to be acceptance of the new reality, no matter how unwanted it may be. Only then can we be open to what God has next for us.

Interestingly, a few months after that sermon Kent led a trip to Israel. On that trip he met a woman and they began dating. Eight months later they got married.

Resurrection, the miracle of new possibilities, doesn't occur without death. We are tempted to bypass the unpleasantness of Holy Week. It's just more appealing to go from waving branches Palm Sunday to shouting "He is risen!" on Easter morning. After all, it's depressing to sit through dark services recounting the betrayal, suffering, and crucifixion of Jesus. It's nice to go from exaltation to exaltation, but life doesn't work that way. There are interruptions to joy. Heartaches happen.

Easter occurs not in spite of death but because of it. Christian faith offers hope because it faces death squarely and moves through it, not around it. It means that pain, disappointment, and heartache are not final realities.

When we can accept the things we cannot change and remain open to God's power to do new things, we discover what resurrection is.

The way some people talk about resurrection, I wonder if many times they mean resuscitation instead. The two are different. Resuscitation means bringing back to life—returning life to the way it was. Resurrection means a whole new life, a different life. I wonder if many times what we really want is resuscitation.

Easter occurs not in spite of death
but because of it.

We want God to restore a relationship. We want God to make a boyfriend or girlfriend come back. We want God to make a spouse return. We want a job back, an old life back, something back the way it was. It's like the joke about what happens when you play a country song in reverse. You get your car back, your wife back, your house back, and so forth. Sometimes we want God to play like a broken record—just return things to the way they used to be!

I went to a new church appointment some years ago in North Carolina. I had been there a few months and stopped by the bank one day to make a deposit. I hadn't met the teller who was helping me, so I introduced myself. I said I was the new pastor at the church just down the street. She looked up and said in a rather somber tone, "Oh, you're him." Now how does one respond to that!

She continued, "I used to go to that church."

"Well, I hope you come back," I told her.

She said, "Can't do it. I liked the former pastor too much. He was wonderful." Then she looked at me and stated, "No one could ever replace him."

I was batting two for two. Of course, since she had never experienced me as a pastor, I reminded myself, *this is not about me!*

"You are exactly right!" I replied. "No one could replace your former pastor. No one ever will. But I hope you will be open to the possibility, whether in this church or somewhere else, that God can bless you as much through another pastor as your former one."

The woman never returned to that church, but I hope she went on to discover a community of faith and pastoral leadership that made her feel as blessed in a new chapter of life as she did in an old one. What a disappointing faith it would be to believe God is not able to do today or tomorrow what God did yesterday. What a sad condition to feel God's best blessings have already been dispensed, that God's blessing power has diminished.

It's so easy to crave resuscitation, isn't it? To want things the way they used to be? To want God to replace a pastor, a church, a spouse, a friend, a job, or a home? But Jesus said, "I am the Resurrection and the Life." He doesn't just restore. He transforms.

Now I realize that he did restore Lazarus. He brought Lazarus back to life. It was, indeed, a resuscitation, but it was also a postponement. Lazarus would die again. His sisters would one day have to relive the loss of death. But when that day came, they would be able to face it with not only a belief but also a trust. The One who is Resurrection and Life works on both sides of the grave.

Death takes away. Death forever changes things. That's what death does, but here is what death cannot do: Death cannot give a future. Death cannot create. Death cannot do a new thing. Only the Great I Am can do that.

The One who is Resurrection and Life works on both sides of the grave.

Once a woman approached me at a conference where I was teaching. She attended a church I once served in that community. She had come to that church under unusual circumstances. She began attending shortly after a reversal of her planned suicide. At home alone she had sat with a pistol beside her, preparing to end her life. Her marriage had failed, and a gambling addiction had wasted her resources; she was out of hope.

As the woman tried to compose a note explaining why she chose to end her life, she heard a voice say, "What are you thinking? You don't want to die." She remembered her niece begging her to attend church with her. The young woman could see that the joy was gone from her aunt's eyes.

The woman made a decision. "I can't go through with this until I honor my niece's request. I owe it to her." She doesn't understand why she had that thought. It didn't make sense at the time; but for whatever reason, she made up her mind not to go through with the suicide until one last visit to church to sit beside her niece.

That Sunday she sat in the last row of seats in the balcony . . . as far away from the front of the church as she could get. A man in the praise team recognized her and knew she used to sing. After the service he found the woman and invited her to join them. She refused but did return to worship the next week. This time she sat on the next to last row in the balcony.

Week after week the woman returned, each time sitting a row closer; eventually working her way to the main floor and toward the front. People in the praise team kept inviting until she gave in and agreed to join them. Sometime during these weeks something happened. It was like an unexpected peace. She met the One who is Resurrection and Life. She decided she wanted to live.

This woman grew up in church. She believed in the Resurrection, but in this chapter of life she found a whole new reason to trust. Christ was no longer just someone to *believe in* but someone to *believe.*

When I talked to the woman at that conference, she flashed her hand at me. A dazzling ring adorned her finger. She had met someone and fallen in love. They were engaged. It's an amazing thing to look in someone's eyes and see them sparkle, knowing that life nearly ended in a flash.

You could say her old life did end. It had to. Her life, as she knew it, had to end in order for the new one to emerge. She couldn't see it. She couldn't even believe it. She just came to a point where she trusted the One who could.

Jesus didn't say, "I can give you resurrection and life." If he had, we would probably be chasing him as fast as that crowd around the lake after he multiplied fish and loaves. Instead he said, "I am the Resurrection and the Life." He is New Life. We find it in him. We experience it in the God we can know.

THE GOD WE CAN KNOW

I hope and pray that examining the "I Am" sayings of Jesus together in this book has provided a fresh awareness that God wants to be revealed to you. God wants to be known. And much more important than knowing *about* God is *knowing God.*

The more we know the great I AM, the better we can finish our own I ams. We are not just made by God but made out of God.

The more we know the one who said, "I am the Bread of Life," the greater satisfaction and joy we have. The more we know the one who said, "I am the Good Shepherd," the greater our security and confidence.

The more we know the one who said, "I am the Light of the World," the more we experience God's guidance and direction.

The more we know the one who said, "I am the True Vine," the more connected we are to God's power. The more we know the one who said, "I am the Way, the Truth, and the Life," the more we walk a pattern for living that gives peace and hope.

The more we know the one who said, "I am the Resurrection and the Life," the more we discover God's possibilities for living.

If you have read this book as part of a group study and have experienced new levels of faith in that community, continue to gather and look for further ways to stay connected and growing. If the spiritual practices have been meaningful and helpful, continue to use these as a means of grace to aid your connection to Christ.

My goal is that you would be inspired by the person of Jesus, experience his presence in new ways, and come to this study's close with a deeper desire to live as a faithful disciple of Jesus Christ.

And this is eternal life, that they may know you,
the only true God, and Jesus Christ whom you have sent.

JOHN 17:3

Reflection/Discussion Questions

Why do you think the raising of Lazarus caused so much alarm for the religious establishment, so much so that they not only wanted to kill Jesus but Lazarus too?

When was the first time you encountered death? What questions or fears did it raise? How did it impact your understanding of God?

Like each of the preceding "I Am" sayings, Jesus' words "I am the Resurrection and the Life" came in the midst of a dialogue. Knowing what led to his being in Bethany and the conversation with Mary, what do you think Jesus wanted Mary to feel and know?

Does exchanging the word trust *for* believe *in this story give you different insight?*

Thinking of the Karl Barth story, have you ever put your trust in God in a way that was like clinging to a rope?

Consider the difference between Lazarus and Jesus. Lazarus was brought back to this life; Jesus was brought back to a resurrected life. What is the difference between resuscitation *and* resurrection *to you?*

When have you experienced some kind of death in order for God to give you new life?

NOTES

_____

_____

_____

_____

_____

_____

_____

_____

_____

_____

_____

_____

_____

_____

_____

_____

_____

_____

_____

_____

_____

_____

_____

Notes

Chapter 1

1. Everett Fox, *The Five Books of Moses: Genesis, Exodus, Leviticus, Numbers, Deuteronomy* (*The Schocken Bible, Volume 1*) (New York: Schocken Books, 2000), xxix.

2. Gail R. O'Day in Leander E. Keck, ed., *The New Interpreter's Bible* Vol. IX (Nashville, TN: Abingdon Press, 1996), 601.

Chapter 2

1. Jean Zornes, "I Am the Bread of Life," *Discipleship Journal,* Issue 120 (Nov/Dec 2000), 64.

2. C. S. Lewis, *Surprised by Joy: The Shape of My Early Life* (New York: Harcourt, Brace Jovanovich, 1966), 170.

3. Steve Beard, "Faith on the Chopping Block," *Good News* Magazine (Nov/Dec 2012), 6.

Chapter 3

1. Tony Campolo, *Let Me Tell You a Story: Life Lessons from Unexpected Places and Unlikely People* (Nashville, TN: Thomas Nelson, 2000), 21–22.

2. Allison Griffin, "George Wallace Jr. Reflects on Father in New Book." December 27, 2011. http://www.military.com/off-duty/books/2011/12/27/george-wallace-jr-reflects-on-father-in-new-book.html (accessed January 18, 2014).

Chapter 4

1. W. Phillip Keller, *A Shepherd Looks at Psalm 23* (Grand Rapids, MI: Zondervan, 2007), 28.

2. R. Kent Hughes and Barbara Hughes, *Liberating Ministry from the Success Syndrome* (Wheaton, IL: Crossway Books, 2009), 69.

3. David Haley, "Fear No Evil: Psalm 23," *Skokie Central Church Sermons* (blog), April 21, 2013. http://skokiecentralchurch.wordpress.com/2013/04/21/2013-04-21-fear-no-evil-psalm-23/ (accessed January 18, 2014).

Chapter 5

1. https://www.youtube.com/watch?v=ED4WtBhZyB0&list=PL54B53ACDFC656FB2&index=1

2. Mike Yaconelli, *Messy Spirituality: God's Annoying Love for Imperfect People* (Grand Rapids, MI: Zondervan, 2002), 63–64, 75–77.

Chapter 6

1. Gail R. O'Day in Leander E. Keck, ed., *The New Interpreter's Bible* Vol. IX (Nashville, TN: Abingdon Press, 1996), 744.

2. Philip Yancey, *What's So Amazing about Grace?* (Grand Rapids, MI: Zondervan, 1997), 45.

3. Rob Bell, *Love Wins: A Book about Heaven, Hell, and the Fate of Every Person Who Ever Lived* (New York: HarperOne, 2012), 154–55.

4. Dallas Willard, *The Spirit of the Disciplines: Understanding How God Changes Lives* (Grand Rapids, MI: Zondervan, 1999), 186.

5. Dallas Willard, *The Great Omission: Reclaiming Jesus's Essential Teachings on Discipleship* (New York: HarperOne, 2006), 133.

Chapter 7

1. Barbara Brown Taylor, *God in Pain: Teaching Sermons on Suffering* (Nashville, TN: Abingdon Press, 1998), 68.

2. F. F. Bruce, *Romans* (Grand Rapids, MI: Eerdmans, 1985), 58.

ABOUT THE AUTHOR

Rob Fuquay serves as senior pastor at St. Luke's United Methodist Church in Indianapolis, one of the largest churches in the denomination. Prior to 2011 he served several congregations, both large and small, in North Carolina. Rob earned degrees from Pfeiffer University in Misenheimer, North Carolina, and from Candler School of Theology at Emory University in Atlanta. He loves the outdoors and enjoys hiking, climbing, and golf. Rob and his wife, Susan, are avid sports fans. They are the parents of three daughters, Julie, Sarah, and Anna.

The God We Can Know
Family of Resources

Join with others on the journey to know God! Rob Fuquay's video introductions to the seven "I Am" sayings will get small groups thinking and talking.

Guides for adult, youth, and children's groups make a churchwide worship and study focus on *The God We Can Know* possible in your faith community.

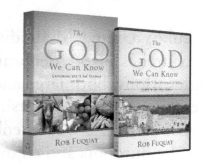

Book ISBN 978-0-8358-1338-9 $9.99
DVD with Group Guide Set ISBN 978-0-8358-1362-4 $39.99
includes Leader's Guides for Adult, Youth, and Children
To order
1-800-972-0433
Bookstore.UpperRoom.org

Visit **www.TheGodWeCanKnow.com** *for additional helps to launch a churchwide study.*

CPSIA information can be obtained
at www.ICGtesting.com
Printed in the USA
LVHW061206150723
752584LV00043B/919